DEDICATION

*To the Chefs and
restaurateurs of Banff and
Lake Louise
who made this book possible*

FOREWORD & ACKNOWLEDGEMENTS

The idea for this book arose one evening while enjoying yet another superb meal at a Rocky Mountain restaurant. Perhaps it was some mysterious short circuit between my palate and my curiousity that did it, but I suddenly started wondering about who was at the source of these delights and what gastronomic magic they were conjuring to create them. This book, a tribute to the chefs and restaurateurs of Banff, Lake Louise and the mountains, is the natural result of that most inspiring meal.

I would like to take this opportunity to thank the many people who made this book possible:

— the chefs, who took such care in creating this array of recipes and then went on to share them with us all;

— the restaurateurs and their friendly staffs, who have created the environments and atmospheres in which such culinary arts can be nurtured and enjoyed;

— the friendly folks at the Archives of the Canadian Rockies who helped me discover Banff's colourful dining history;

— my wife Ingrid, and Scott Rowed and Chip DeRoo, who offered encouragement, enthusiasm, moral support and untold hours of help in gathering the contributions and preparing the manuscript;

— and Susan Hammond, Nancy MacEachern, Lori Fitzgerald and Lesley Cook, who offered helpful editorial comments and their proof reading skills to the project.

The end result, I hope, is a book that truly serves up 'A Taste of Banff'.

Douglas Leighton

TABLE OF CONTENTS

*". . . at the Lux Theatre . . . the star . . . is an automobile mechanic.
He has big ideas . . . Then the end of the world is predicted. And
he falls in love. Then comes — but that would be telling!"*

                    Banff Crag and Canyon, May 29, 1925

BREAKFAST

PRODUCTS OF CALEDONIA MINERAL SPRINGS

	HALF PINTS	PINTS
MAGI "SALINE" WATER, SPARKLING - - - -	.15	.25
DUNCAN "APERIENT" WATER, SPARKLING - - -	.25	

Casaba Melon with Lemon 25   **B. C. Berries with Cream 35**
Cantaloupe (Half) 25   **Sliced Peaches with Cream 35**
STEWED PRUNES WITH CREAM 25   ORANGE JUICE 30
BANANA, SLICED WITH CREAM 25   ORANGE, WHOLE 15, SLICED 20
STEWED FIGS WITH CREAM 25

CEREALS WITH MILK 20; WITH CREAM 30

Grilled or Fried Whitefish 65
Fish Cakes 40, with Bacon 50

Broiled or Fried Spring Chicken (Half) $1.25 (20 minutes)
BROILED SIRLOIN STEAK 1.60   FRIED SMALL STEAK 1.00
BACON (THREE) STRIPS 35, (SIX) STRIPS 65   BROILED HAM 65
LAMB CHOPS (ONE) 45, (TWO) 80
HAM AND FRIED EGGS 65   BACON AND FRIED EGGS 65
ONE STRIP BACON SERVED WITH OTHER ORDERS 15

Fried Fresh Tomatoes with Bacon 60
Omelet with Green Peppers and Chopped Chicken 60

EGGS

BOILED (ONE) 20, (TWO) 35   SCRAMBLED 35   FRIED (ONE) 20, (TWO) 35
POACHED ON TOAST (ONE) 20, (TWO) 40
OMELETS: PLAIN 45   JELLY, HAM OR SPANISH 60

POTATOES: FRENCH FRIED OR HASHED BROWNED 25   LYONNAISE POTATOES 25

BREAD AND BUTTER SERVICE PER PERSON
TOAST 15   HOT ROLLS 15   BRAN OR CORN MUFFINS 15
WHITE, BROWN AND RAISIN BREAD 10

Griddle Cakes with Maple Syrup 30

PRESERVED FRUITS, MARMALADE, JAMS OR JELLIES 25
(IN INDIVIDUAL JARS)
STRAWBERRIES   CHERRIES   PEACHES   PINEAPPLE   RASPBERRIES
QUINCE JELLY   CRAB APPLE JELLY
STRAWBERRY JAM   PRUNES   RASPBERRY JAM
ORANGE OR GRAPEFRUIT MARMALADE

PRESERVED FIGS 40

TEA, COFFEE, ETC.

COFFEE, POT 20 (SERVED WITH HOT MILK OR CREAM)   TEA, POT 20
INSTANT POSTUM 20   COCOA, CUP 20, POT 25
INDIVIDUAL SEALED BOTTLE MILK 15   "HORLICK'S MALTED MILK" 20

WAITERS ARE FORBIDDEN TO ACCEPT OR SERVE VERBAL ORDERS

PASSENGERS ARE REQUESTED TO INSPECT MEAL CHECK BEFORE MAKING PAYMENT, AND
IN CASE OF ANY OVERCHARGE OR UNSATISFACTORY SERVICE, REPORT THE MATTER TO THE
STEWARD IN CHARGE OF CAR OR TO
W. A. COOPER,
MANAGER, SLEEPING AND DINING CARS
MONTREAL.

2-8-E. 7-8 18-8-23-V.
1-8-W.

Canadian Pacific Railway Dining Car
Breakfast Menu, 1923

A History:
'Where Mousse Meets Moose'

When one thinks of the Canadian Rockies, it is usually visions of mountain majesty, emerald forests, sparkling lakes and abundant wildlife that come dancing through one's head. But since Banff and Lake Louise first burst on to the international tourism scene 100 years ago, fine dining has always played a vital role in their appeal. Born a luxurious Victorian mountain adventure, they have matured to become world class resorts with culinary offerings to match.

For most of the past 10,000 years, the Banff dining scene was rather primitive. Small bands of Stone Age peoples wandered through, hunting game and gathering the seasonal crops of roots and berries. Sitting around an evening hearth after a big hunt or harvest and nibbling on bison ribs and berries was one of their greatest pleasures. And when camped at the hot pools above the Bow River, such feasts topped off by soothing soaks was Indian life at its most luxurious.

Until just over a century ago, the Indians — most recently the Stoney tribe — enjoyed this rare delight in splendid seclusion. But then came a trickle of white men, exploring, trapping and probing the mountains for shining stones. A few found the hot pools, savoured a good dip, and then moved on leaving little sign of their passing. But in 1883, a great steel snake, with a head of fire and iron, came out of the east and pierced this wilderness primeval. The Canadian Pacific Railroad, and civilization, had arrived.

That fall William Van Horne, the CPR manager, came riding the rails westward to inspect the end of the line. One glance at Van Horne would confirm that here was a man who enjoyed food. Tall and 'massively built', his appetite was 'in defiance of all accepted precepts of moderation'; he was known to devour a pound of caviar in a single sitting! As he crossed the prairies, his thoughts drifted to food. Not food for his own well rounded frame but rather meals for the passengers who would soon be travelling the CPR line. Dining cars were just fine for flat country, but when it came to crossing the high passes of the Rockies, their extra weight would be too much of a burden. Dining stops along the way seemed the logical solution.

Although Van Horne had considered the problems of the mountains, it was not until he saw them that he realized their blessings. These crags were an obstacle of incredible beauty and a potential tourism resource of international calibre. Reasoning that 'If you can't export the scenery, you have to import the tourists', he recognized that to attract the tourists of the day — the wealthy upper classes of eastern Canada, the US and Europe — his line would have to offer the luxury accommodation and quality cuisine to which they were accustomed. And soon his creative mind had transformed his simple dining stop plan into a vision of sumptuous mountain resorts. But with so many beautiful spots to choose from, where should they be built?

Just as Van Horne was pondering this problem, three CPR construction workers were about to help him make his most important choice. Out prospecting one cool November day, they stumbled upon a 'wonder of wonders', the hot springs on the slopes of Sulphur Mountain. When word of this treasure finally got back to Ottawa two years later, Van Horne started smiling. In the golden age of fashionable European spa resorts, here was the makings of the ultimate Rocky Mountain resort just off the CPR line. Applying his considerable political clout, Van Horne soon had the federal government proposing to protect the hot springs against 'private' (other than CPR, that is!) development. On November 28, 1885, Canada's first national park reserve was formally established around the hot springs at Banff (so named in honour of the CPR President's native Banffshire in Scotland). And before the ink was dry on this landmark legislation, the plans for the first Banff Springs Hotel (and the first lodge at Lake Louise) were being drawn up. In the spring of 1888 the Banff Springs Hotel, rising out of the pine woods like some misplaced castle, opened its doors to the world's travelling class.

Tally-ho in front of original Banff Springs Hotel, ca. 1912
- George Noble Photograph

As for the local Stoneys, one can only imagine the culture shock that they must have experienced when they found their hunting grounds invaded by the Victorian world at its most extravagant. The Banff Springs Hotel was some teepee! And from it came strange people who sneered at an offering of delicious roast bear paw and soaked in the hot pools with their clothes on! Confusing though all this must have been for the natives, it didn't take some of them long to catch on to the white man's ways. Watching them gain free train rides in 1895, writer Douglas Sladen noted that they 'were always sharp enough not to understand tickets'.

By the turn of the century, the Banff Springs was recognized as one of the best hotels in Canada and one of the top mountain resorts on the continent. It was the crown jewel of the CPR's elegant 'Europe to the Orient' transcontinental dining service, a system so refined that each egg, produced by a farm along the route, was dated to ensure freshness. With exclusive French service and a menu fit for a king — for royalty, the rich and the famous were part of the clientele — the Banff Springs changed Banff from another bush camp of bacon and beans to a gourmet's oasis in the heart of the wilderness.

But there was more being poached in Banff than just
fashionable breakfast eggs. Despite increasing official
protection, much of the local wildlife was still ending up
on the dinner table. It was, after all, a frontier tradition. And
no self respecting mountain man was about to let some
government city slicker tell him that he couldn't go hunting
... especially when a lot of other city slickers, when the
pesky park wardens weren't looking, would pay him good
wages to take them out to do just that! In the end, the park
officials did manage to get poaching under control; they
gave up trying to catch some of the more wily poachers
and hired them on as wardens to catch the others.

The tradition of wild game dining lived on, however, and
influenced by Banff's sophisticated visitors, evolved into a
unique blend of frontier and gourmet cooking. At the King
Edward Hotel, a popular spot for local mountain folk and
those there to rub shoulders with 'real cowboys', the 1910
Christmas Dinner menu featured such rare delights as
Moose Nose and Tongue with Mushrooms, Roast Bear with
Black Currant Jelly and Haunch of Mountain Sheep.
Luckily for the wildlife, new game regulations soon brought
this colourful culinary era to a close.

Postcard scene of Banff Avenue, ca 1914
- Coast Publishing Co. Photograph

Mountaineers on first ascent of Mount Lefroy, 1897
- Tom Wilson Jr. collection

For many adventurous visitors, a trip to Banff was a chance to explore the mountains. The traditional trail fare of bannock and bacon was still a staple (bacon was so revered as a frontier food that an early Crag and Canyon editorial, titled 'Bacon and Civilization', was devoted solely to its virtues) but modern foods soon supplemented the wilderness diet. Of special note were dried foods, which promised to be ideal for such expeditions. Unfortunately, these early versions of today's backcountry favourites had their problems. As Mary T.S. Schaffer warned in 1907, ". . . beware of the dried cabbage; no fresh air in existence will ever blow off sufficient of the odour to let it get safely to the mouth . . . and to this day I wonder if that dried milk had ever seen a cow, or if any hen would acknowledge the motherhood of those dried eggs".

In the years leading to the First World War, Banff blossomed with the boisterous innocence of the era. Well within the accepted range of frontier truthstretching, the Banff Crag and Canyon editor boasted that 'Banff is the most cosmopolitan place in Canada'. It was a playground for the upper crust, a place for tea and Tally-ho rides, leisurely hot pool soaks and elegant evening dinners. Most still arrived by train but by 1910, the pioneering Calgary Auto Club had sputtered into town to bring in a new age.

Staff 'Hard Times' Dance, Chateau Lake Louise, 1912
- Tom Wilson Jr. Collection

Cafes sprung up in town as Banff's popularity soared and 'the proprietors of the new eating places were tickled with the rush of trade'. The story of one of these proprietors, a black man named Bill Davies, sums up the rollicking good spirit of the times. In an era of rampant racism, when some restaurants were advertising their allegedly superior practice of hiring 'all white help', Bill hired a Chinese cook and a young Indian helper and operated the 'White Help Cafe'.

The Roaring Twenties really roared into the resorts of the Rockies. At the Banff Springs and the Chateau Lake Louise, the carefree mood of the times reached extravagant heights. Their dining rooms were filled with 'everybody who's anybody', sipping champagne and enjoying such specialties as Slice of Sirloin 'Bow Valley', Julienne of Sole 'Mount Victoria' and Eggs 'Lac Miroir' created by top European chefs and served with impeccable style. With their outrageously elegant decor and palatial settings, these CPR dining rooms, in this golden age of their rarified exclusiveness, were truly bastions of unabashed snobbery.

But behind the scenes at these CPR castles, there was a much different flavour. Aside from the professional chefs and waiters (the latter were, by the way, enjoying the golden age of tips), the huge staffs were made up mostly of young people from far and wide, here for summer jobs and plenty of good times. It was a cherished opportunity to work at these resorts and move among movie stars and magnates; and the staff, in their own way, had at least as much fun as their pampered guests.

Back in the more casual atmosphere of Banff, there was dining at the Cascade, King Edward and Mount Royal hotels and a handful of independent cafes. After dinner spots included the Cascade Hall, for the 'best dance music in Alberta, and the Lux Theatre, for such film 'classics' as "The Bohemian Girl" (Basil Horsfall's Latest Sensation!) or "Arizona Wildcat", starring Tom Mix and Tony, 'The Wonder Horse'; plus the odd pie-eating contest.

It was a grand time for all. Then came the Great Depression, which thinned out the crowds even at the CPR palaces, followed by World War Two, which really took the wind out of Banff's sails. But only for a while.

In the post-war era, a new Banff came to life. In the age of the automobile and increasing affluence, it became a resort not just for the wealthy but for everyone. And with the development of superb ski areas nearby, it soon became a year round destination.

Despite these changes, Banff maintained its fashionable mystique — the rich and famous still visit — while evolving to satisfy the varied palates of today's visitors. The tradition of fine dining, once the preserve of the grand hotels, has permeated the scene. Inspired by the aristocratic elegance of the Banff Springs and the Chateau Lake Louise (whose atmospheres remain unforgettable experiences) and the culinary perfection of Le Beaujolais (one of Canada's premier restaurants), the Banff and Lake Louise dining scene has become an inspirational part of today's Rocky Mountain experience. Reflecting their stature as internationally renowned resorts, their restaurants offer a smorgasbord of delectable delights. From sophisticated European cuisine to gourmet Mexican dishes, from Japanese Sushi Bars to Canadian buffalo fondues, here is a diverse selection of authentic international dishes and some deliciously surprising combinations. Served in black tie to blue jean atmospheres and spiced with entertainment to taste, it is easy to see why 'dining out' is Banff's most popular pastime.

One can be sure that William Van Horne would be most satisfied with the way his mountain dining stops have evolved. But considering his legendary palate, it is perhaps a good thing for Canadian history that it took the Rocky Mountain dining scene 100 years to reach today's epicurean heights. Had such a diversity of delicacies been served here in Van Horne's time, he might never have managed to pull away from the tables long enough to finish his national railway.

Facing Page: Banff, Winter Evening
Douglas Leighton Photograph

THE
RECIPES

ON ROCKY MOUNTAIN RECIPES

The recipes contained in this book have been perfected specifically for the high altitudes of the Rockies. When preparing some of these dishes at home, some cooking times will have to be adjusted to your elevation. It should also be remembered that different stoves have varying real temperatures (don't totally trust that dial!). The first time you create one of these delicious tastes of Banff, keep a close watch and fine tune the recipe to your kitchen.

The town of Banff sits at an elevation of 4500 ft (1400 m) and Lake Louise (at the lake) is at 5500 ft (1700 m), for an average working elevation of 5000 ft (1525 m). Compared to sea level, at such altitudes water boils at a lower temperature — thus boiling water is actually cooler — and cooking times for processes involving liquids are proportionately longer. A one minute egg at sea level is a two minute egg in Banff (and a four minute egg on the almost 10,000 ft (3000 m) summit of nearby Mt. Rundle, should you happen to be up there for breakfast). In general, when cooking at lower elevations, times for Banff recipes involving liquids should be shortened.

The lower air pressures at higher elevations also mean faster evaporation. Foods cooked in Banff will lose moisture more rapidly than those cooked at sea level; as such, less liquids are required for preparing Banff recipes at lower elevations. As a guideline, decrease liquids by 2 to 3 tablespoons for each cup called for when preparing a Banff recipe at sea level.

Still another effect of lower air pressures is that the gases in baked goods will expand more rapidly than at sea level. To compensate, when preparing Banff baking recipes at sea level, increase baking soda or powder by about 1/4 teaspoon for each teaspoon required, increase sugar by about 2 to 3 tablespoons for each cup called for, beat the eggs vigorously, and decrease oven temperatures by about 25°F (15°C). And don't forget to adjust the liquids as well: a moist cake recipe in Banff can become a mush cake recipe at sea level!

A little experimentation will usually be required to create perfect results in your home kitchen. But then, besides the eating, that's the fun part of cooking anyway!

ENTRÉES

'Where it all began',
CPR Dining Car 'Buckingham', 1894
Vaux Family Photograph

Fetturcine Alfredo p. 41

CONTENTS

GARITHES UVESTI
(Shrimp Casserole)

serves four

butterfly shrimp, cleaned	16 oz (450 g)
feta cheese, crumbled	8 oz (225 g)
Romano cheese, grated	5 tbsp (75 ml)
large onion, diced	1
green onions, chopped	1 bunch
fresh parsley, chopped	1 bunch
garlic, diced	8 to 10 cloves
dry white wine	1 cup (250 ml)
tomato purée	1 14 oz (400 ml) can
water	2 to 3 cups (500 to 750 ml)
vegetable oil	3 tbsp (45 ml)
salt	
black pepper	

*To prepare sauce sauté onion, green onions and garlic in oil
in medium to large pan. Add parsley and wine to mixture
and bring to boil for 5 minutes. Stir in water,
tomato purée and salt and pepper to taste. Boil rapidly to
reduce liquid by about 1/3 to thicken. If desired, corn starch
can be added to thicken sauce also.
Divide shrimp into 4 portions and place in 4 small
casserole dishes. Add sauce and crumbled feta cheese and
sprinkle with Romano cheese. Bake at 375°F (190°C)
for 20 to 30 minutes and serve.*

Jason Karlos
Chef
BALKAN VILLAGE RESTAURANT

"I am DEE-LIGHTED with your town."

*former US President Teddy Roosevelt,
visiting Banff in 1915*

SOUVLAKI
(WITH PITA BREAD AND TZATZIKI SAUCE)

serves four to six

pork tenderloin	2 lb (900 g)
medium tomatoes	2
medium to large onion	½
pita bread	1 package

Cut pork tenderloin into 1 inch (2.5 cm) cubes and marinate overnight in a mix of:

olive oil	2 cups (500 ml)
lemon juice	¼ cup (60 ml)
salt	
black pepper	
oregano	

For Tzatziki sauce:

plain yogurt	2 cups (500 ml)
medium English cucumber, grated and well strained	1
garlic, well crushed	4 to 5 cloves
olive oil	3 tbsp (45 ml)
red wine vinegar	1 tbsp (15 ml)
salt	
black pepper	

Mix all ingredients thoroughly using a spoon, not a mixer. Refrigerate for about 2 hours.

Dice tomatoes and onion. Put pork cubes on skewer and barbecue until well done, basting occasionally with left over marinade.
On a pita bread place about 2 tbsp (30 ml) of Tzatziki sauce and a sprinkling of diced tomato and onion.
Remove barbecued pork from skewer and place on top.
Roll pita bread around this and serve.

Jason Karlos
Chef
BALKAN VILLAGE RESTAURANT

VEGETABLE STRUDEL

serves four

onion, finely diced	1 cup (250 ml)
carrot, finely diced	3 cups (750 ml)
cauliflower, finely diced	1½ cups (375 ml)
broccoli, finely diced	1½ cups (375 ml)
cheddar cheese, grated	1½ cups (375 ml)
vegetable oil	½ cup (125 ml)
eggs	2
phyllo pastry	½ package
butter	6 tbsp (90 ml)
garlic, minced	2 tbsp (30 ml)
oregano	2 tbsp (30 ml)
dill	2 tbsp (30 ml)
basil	1½ tbsp (20 ml)
salt	1 tbsp (15 ml)
black pepper	

Sauté onion with garlic in 2 tbsp (30 ml) of butter until softened, not browned. Drain and let cool.
Beat eggs and combine with sautéed mixture, vegetables, cheese and spices.
Over low heat, combine remaining butter with oil.
On a damp cloth place a sheet of phyllo pastry and working quickly, brush the pastry with butter and oil mix. Place another sheet of pastry over the first and brush again with butter and oil mixture. Repeat until 10 pastry sheets have been done.
Spoon vegetable mixture onto the centre of the pastry, making a long mound. Using the cloth underneath fold the pastry over the vegetable mixture. Then roll onto a baking sheet with the seam down and tuck the ends under the strudel. Brush with butter and oil mixture and bake at 350°F (180°C) for about 1 hour or until pastry is nicely browned. Remove from oven and let cool for a few minutes before slicing. Serve with a cheese sauce.

BANFF PARK LODGE

SNAPPER GRENOBLOISE

serves two

fillets of red snapper	2
lemons	2
capers	2 tbsp (30 ml)
croutons	½ cup (125 ml)
butter	⅓ cup (80 ml)

Peel and section lemons, removing all membrane and seeds. Melt butter over medium heat in a skillet. Add snapper fillets and lightly brown on one side. Turn fillets and add lemon, capers and croutons. Transfer to 400°F (200°C) oven and finish cooking until fish flakes to the touch and the croutons have absorbed all the butter.

Laura Buckley
Chef
BANFF ROCKY
MOUNTAIN RESORT

"... *she always moved with much grace, this charming waitress ... She waltzed in with a cup of tea, she waltzed out with an empty dish, and some of us got to keeping time with her motions ... we called her 'The Waltzing Waitress'.*"

on dining in Banff, Edward Roper, 1911, in 'By Track and Trail: A Journey Through Canada'

MUSSELS IN TOMATO AND GARLIC BROTH

serves 6

fresh mussels in shell	3 lb (1.5 kg)
olive oil	3 tbsp (45 ml)
onions, chopped	2½ oz (75 g)
garlic cloves, chopped and crushed	3
celery, finely sliced	1½ oz (45 g)
tomatoes, peeled, seeded and diced	6
white wine	2 cups (500 ml)
salt	
pepper	
chopped parsley	

*Clean mussels with kitchen knife (shells have to be closed
to ensure freshness), wash in cold water and drain.
Heat olive oil in a pot large enough to hold all of the mussels.
Add onions and garlic, sauté to a golden colour,
then add celery and tomatoes and put on high heat.
Place the mussels in the pot with about ⅓ of the wine
and a little salt and fresh ground pepper. Cover the pot
tightly to keep the steam in so that the mussels will open up.
When the mussels are open pour in the rest of the wine,
season to taste and bring to a boil. Do not overcook
the mussels or they will shrink and become tough.
Before serving, toss the mussels to mix ingredients.
Serve in a pre-warmed dish. Sprinkle with chopped parsley.
Empty mussel shells can be used as eating tools for
mussels and broth.*

Martin Luthi
Executive Chef
BANFF SPRINGS HOTEL

*"According to those who know best, between 50 and 10,000 autos
arrived in town yesterday . . ."*

Banff Crag and Canyon, August 4, 1917

REINDEER EMINCEE WITH CRANBERRIES AND MUSHROOMS

serves 6

Reindeer hip or veal Emincee (thinly sliced)	27 oz (750 g)
chanterelles or fresh mushrooms	7 oz (200 g)
oil	2 tbsp (30 ml)
butter	1 oz (30 g)
onions, chopped	1 oz (30 g)
dry white wine	12½ oz (350 ml)
brandy	2 tbsp (30 ml)
cream (half liquid, half whipped)	12½ oz (350 ml)
cranberries	4 oz (115 g)
butter	2 oz (60 g)
flour	1 oz (30 g)

*In a shallow pan, heat oil, add sliced meat and brown evenly.
Place meat in a strainer over bowl to retain juices.
Using same pan, sauté mushrooms, onions and cranberries
in 1 oz (30 g) of butter. Place in separate dish.
Deglaze pan using white wine and brandy, stirring to
dissolve drippings. Make a paste of butter and flour and
add this to liquid — stir constantly until slightly thickened.
Simmer for 5 minutes. Add meat juice. Mix in the
liquid cream and then slowly fold in the whipped cream.
Season with salt and pepper to taste. Add all other
ingredients — heat quickly but do not boil.
Serve on pre-warmed plate.*

Martin Luthi
Executive Chef
BANFF SPRINGS HOTEL

"Only fast thinkers become leaders. He who hesitates is bossed."

Banff Crag and Canyon, April 17, 1923

LE CARRE D'AGNEAU 'PROVENCALE'
(Rack of lamb)

serves two

rack of lamb, trimmed	26 oz (750 g)
shallots, finely chopped	2
fresh parsley, chopped	3 tbsp (45 ml)
small garlic cloves, minced	3
dried thyme, crumbled	1 tsp (5 ml)
fresh bread crumbs	½ cup (125 ml)
unsalted butter	2 tbsp (30 ml)
salt	¼ tsp (1 ml)
freshly ground black pepper	¼ tsp (1 ml)
demi-glaze sauce	½ cup (125 ml)
watercress sprigs	

*In a mixing bowl, combine the shallots, parsley, garlic
and thyme. Melt the butter and add, tossing the mixture well
with a fork.*
*Sprinkle the lamb with salt and pepper to taste. Heat a large
skillet over high heat and brown the lamb, turning it to
brown all sides as evenly as possible. Transfer the lamb
rack flesh side up to a roasting pan and pour off all the
fat from the skillet.*
*With the demi-glaze sauce, deglaze the skillet over
a high heat — scraping up any brown bits — for 30 seconds.
Then strain the sauce through a fine sieve into a
small saucepan. Set aside and keep warm.*
*Pat the herb mixture evenly over the top of the rack of lamb.
Put the lamb in a pre-heated 450°F (230°C) oven for about
15 minutes to cook medium rare.*
*Transfer lamb to a plate and let it stand, uncovered,
on top of the stove or some other warm place for 10 to 15
minutes. Place lamb on cutting board and slice the rack
between the ribs to make chops. Serve with demi-glaze sauce
and garnish with watercress sprigs.*

Gerhard Frey
Chef
LE BEAUJOLAIS

LES PAUPIETTES DE SOLE
ET SAUMON AU SAFFRON
(Sole wrapped with Salmon)

serves two

filets of dover sole	8
salmon, 1 inch (2.5 cm) cubes	8
tomatoes	2
echalote (shallot onion)	1
garlic clove	1
dry white wine	3½ oz (100 ml)
whipping cream	3½ oz (100 ml)
butter	1 oz (30 g)
basil	
saffron	
salt	
pepper	

Wrap the salmon cubes with the sole filets and use a toothpick to hold them together.
Peel the tomatoes (use hot water) and cut into small cubes.
Chop the echalote and garlic very fine and saute in butter in a large skillet. Then place the paupiettes (salmon wrapped in sole) in the skillet, add the wine and poach for about 2 minutes. Remove the paupiettes, slice them in half and arrange on a lightly buttered service plate. Keep warm.
Add saffron and basil to taste to the pan mix and let simmer for about 2 minutes. Add whipping cream and let simmer until thickened. Add salt and pepper to taste.
Pour sauce over paupiettes and garnish with tomato cubes.

Gerhard Frey
Chef
LE BEAUJOLAIS

"The student of human nature will find many subjects of interest on the trails in and out of Banff."

Banff Crag and Canyon, July 14, 1912

CANADIAN MOUNTAIN STEW

serves six to eight

stewing beef, cubed	3 lb (1½ kg)
water	8 cups (2 l)
beef gravy base	4 oz (115 g)
flour	3 oz (85 g)
carrots, cubed	1½ cup (375 ml)
celery, cubed	1½ cup (375 ml)
onion, cubed	1½ cup (375 ml)
turnip, cubed	1½ cup (375 ml)
potato, cubed	1½ cup (375 ml)
whole mushrooms, canned or fresh	1 cup (250 ml)
red wine	½ cup (125 ml)
paprika	¼ tsp (1 ml)
oregano	¼ tsp (1 ml)
black pepper	¼ tsp (1 ml)
basil	¼ tsp (1 ml)
thyme	¼ tsp (1 ml)
bay leaf	1

In a large pot over a high heat, brown meat until cooked completely through. Reduce heat to medium. Stir in flour and allow to cook into beef cubes.
In another pot, add beef base to water and bring to boil. Add to meat and stir until flour is well mixed in. Skim off any fat or flour lumps from surface. Add the vegetables, except for the potatoes, and cook on a medium heat until about half done. Add the potatoes and spices and simmer until vegetables are cooked through. Then add the red wine and mushrooms. Simmer for about 5 minutes. If further thickening is desired, stir in a mixture of 2 tbsp (30 ml) flour and 2 tbsp (30 ml) red wine. Remove bay leaf and serve immediately.

BUMPER'S
THE BEEF HOUSE

"The village dogs seem to have vetoed the order-in-council forbidding them to run at large."

Banff Crag and Canyon, August 22, 1903

CABOOSE CRAB LEGS

serves four

Atlantic snow crab legs	1½ lb (675 g)
large onion, whole, skinned	1
celery stalks	2 or 3
lemon, quartered	1
water	3 qts (3 l)
fresh parsley, finely chopped	
clarified butter, heated	

In a 1 gallon (4.5 l) pot, bring water to boil.
Put onion, celery and lemon in pot and let boil.
Split crab legs and add to boiling pot. Boil vigorously
for about 6 minutes or until crab meat is white and falls
away from the shell. Remove crab legs from pot with tongs,
arrange on a plate, sprinkle lightly with parsley and serve
with hot clarified butter.

CABOOSE
STEAK AND LOBSTER

"Some hungry mortal made a raid on a cargo of beef . . . last night.
Whoever was the culprit, he showed his epicurean propensities by
leisurely cutting out the choicest bits."

Banff Crag and Canyon, Dec. 29, 1901

CURRY GLAZED PORK CHOPS

serves six to eight

pork chops, trimmed	8
large onion, chopped	½
cornstarch	1½ tbsp (20 ml)
brown sugar	2 tbsp (30 ml)
curry powder	1 tbsp (15 ml)
cinnamon	1 tbsp (15 ml)
salt	1 tsp (5 ml)
beef bouillon cube	1
water	1 cup (250 ml)
ketchup	2 tbsp (30 ml)
strained apricots (purée of drained canned apricots)	4 oz (115 g)

Brown chops in a hot pan and season with salt and pepper to taste. Remove and lay in casserole dish.
Add a little oil to the pan and sauté the onions until transparent. Mix cornstarch, sugar, curry powder, cinnamon and salt together and then stir into pan mixture.
Add water and cook until bubbling. Add bouillon cube and stir until dissolved. Stir in ketchup and apricots.
Pour over chops, cover and bake at 350°F (180°C) for about 45 to 50 minutes.
Serve with steamed cauliflower flowerettes with a light cheese sauce or garnished with buttered bread crumbs.

Lynne Grillmair
Chef
Bugaboo Lodge
CANADIAN MOUNTAIN HOLIDAYS

"Oh! she's a hefty feeder,
is the mountain climbing girl!"

from anonymous poem, 'The Mountain Climbing Girl',
Banff Crag and Canyon, Dec. 15, 1900

SPATZLE
('Tiny Dumplings')

all-purpose flour	3 cups (750 ml)
salt	1 tsp (5 ml)
ground nutmeg	¼ tsp (1 ml)
eggs	4
milk	1 cup (250 ml)
bread crumbs	1 cup (250 ml)
butter (optional)	¼ lb (115 g)

In a large mixing bowl, combine flour, nutmeg and ½ tsp (2 ml) of salt. In a small side bowl, beat eggs with fork until smooth. Add eggs to flour mixture and stir in. Add milk, poured in a thin stream, while stirring constantly and stir until dough has a sticky smooth consistency. Put two quarts (2 l) of water and the remaining salt in a large saucepan and bring to a boil. Set a colander with large holes over the saucepan and, a few tablespoons at a time, press the dough through the holes with a spoon so that they fall directly into the boiling water below. Boil briskly for 5 to 8 minutes, and stir occasionally to keep the dumplings from sticking together. Remove when cooked (taste to see if they are tender), cool immediately in ice water, then drain. Over high heat, sauté bread crumbs in butter until light brown. Add spatzle and toss until coated with crumbs. Serve with Sauerbraten or other meat dish.

Jaroslav Nydr
Executive Chef
CHATEAU LAKE LOUISE

"Scientists predict that in 100 years there will be nothing in the world to laugh at. But they're wrong because 100 years from now the people will laugh every time they think of us."

Banff Crag and Canyon, March 7, 1923

SAUERBRATEN
(Bavarian Pot Roast)

serves six to eight

For marinade:

dry red wine	**½ cup (125 ml)**
red wine vinegar	**½ cup (125 ml)**
water	**2 cups (500 ml)**
medium onion, peeled, sliced	**1**
black peppercorns	**5**
whole juniper berries	**4**
small bay leaves	**2**
salt	**1 tsp (5 ml)**

For pot roast:

boneless top or bottom round beef roast (trimmed of fat)	**4 lb (1.8 kg)**
onions, chopped	**½ cup (125 ml)**
carrot, chopped	**½ cup (125 ml)**
celery, chopped	**½ cup (125 ml)**
gingersnap crumbs	**½ cup (125 ml)**
lard	**3 tbsp (45 ml)**
flour	**2 tbsp (30 ml)**
water	**½ cup (125 ml)**

For marinade, first crush peppercorns and juniper berries together and then mix all ingredients together in large saucepan and bring to boil. Let cool.
Put beef in large crock pot and cover with the marinade. (The marinade should cover at least ½ the depth of the roast; if necessary, add more wine.) Turn the roast to moisten all sides. Then cover the pot with aluminum foil or plastic and refrigerate for 3 days, turning the roast over at least twice daily to ensure even distribution of marinade.
After this period, remove the meat from the pot and pat it completely dry with paper towels. Strain the marinade through a fine sieve and set aside.
Over a high heat, melt lard in pot and sear roast, turning frequently to avoid burning, until browned on all sides. Remove meat from pot and set aside.

SAUERBRATEN (Continued)

Lower heat and add onions, carrots and celery,
and cook until soft and light brown. Stir in flour and
stir until flour begins to colour. Then pour in 2 cups
(500 ml) of the saved marinade and ½ cup (125 ml) of water,
bring to a boil, and whisk until smooth.
Return roast to the pot, cover, and let simmer over a low heat
for at least 2 hours or until meat is tender. When done
transfer meat to a platter and keep warm.
Skim fat off top of liquid remaining in pot and bring
to a boil. Either reduce this liquid or add more saved
marinade to give required 2½ cups (625 ml) of liquid
needed for sauce. Reduce heat to medium, add crumbs, and
cook until crumbs disintegrate and sauce thickens.
Strain this liquid through a fine sieve and keep warm.
To serve, slice the roast and moisten slices with sauce.
Put extra sauce in a side dish. Serve with Spatzle.

Jaroslav Nydr
Executive Chef
CHATEAU LAKE LOUISE

"The Canadian Pacific Railway ought to have a commission on
detective cameras, kodaks, hawkeyes, etc. . . . Whenever you stop
at a station, all the steps for getting down are packed with people
taking pot shots with kodaks. American children learn kodaking long
before they learn to behave themselves . . . every operator imagines
he is going to kodak an Indian; but the wily Indian sits in the shade,
where instantaneous photography availeth not, and, if he observes
himself being 'time-exposed' covers his head with a blanket."

Douglas Sladen, 1895,
in 'On the Cars and Off'

GRILLED SALMON
WITH SAUCE GRIBICHE

serves two

Prepare two 8 oz (225 g) salmon fillets by marinating for 24 hours in marinade of:

vegetable oil	sufficient to cover fillets
garlic, minced	4 cloves
lemon, wedges, juice	½
tarragon	1 tbsp (15 ml)
thyme	pinch
bay leaves, crushed	3

Remove fillets from marinade, drain until moist, place on hot grill. Let grill for about 2 minutes per side. Do not overcook. Serve hot on a leaf of green lettuce and garnish with tomato and lemon slices. On the side, serve Sauce Gribiche.

Combine French mayonnaise:

olive oil	¾ cup (185 ml)
egg yolks	2
French mustard	½ tbsp (8 ml)
salt	
pepper	

With:

capers, finely chopped	8
tarragon, finely chopped*	pinch
chervil, finely chopped	pinch
parsley, finely chopped	half a parsley head
egg, hard boiled, with yolk and white separated and then finely chopped	1
lemon, juice from	½
dill pickle, finely chopped	½

*for best results, soak the tarragon for a day in white wine before using.

Patrice Durandeau and
John Mayes
Chefs
DEER LODGE

LEG OF LAMB WITH SPINACH, HAM AND RICOTTA STUFFING

serves six

leg of lamb, bone in	6 lbs (2.7 kg)
cooked ham	3½ oz (100 g)
spinach, blanched	5 oz (140 g)
garlic cloves	2
Ricotta cheese	4 oz (115 g)
salt	
pepper	
nutmeg	
egg yolks	2
bread crumbs	
red wine	3½ oz (100 ml)

Debone leg of lamb (or have butcher do it for you).
Cut ham into small cubes. Finely chop the spinach.
Crush the garlic cloves. In a mixing bowl, combine ham,
spinach, garlic, cheese and salt, pepper and nutmeg to taste
and mix together well. Fold in egg yolks and enough
bread crumbs to loosely bind the mixture.
Fill the lamb leg cavity with the stuffing and tie closed with
a butcherstring. Season the lamb to taste, place in
roasting pan, and roast at 375°F (190°C) for
45 to 50 minutes. After the first 15 minutes of roasting,
pour wine over roast. Continue to baste with wine frequently
until done.

Wolfgang Vogt
Chef
GIORGIO'S

"A number of tourists made the discovery on Friday that showers
in Banff contain considerable wetness."

Banff Crag and Canyon, July 29, 1901

BUFFALO FONDUE

For fondue:

per serving,
buffalo sirloin butt
(or beef substitute)   8 oz (225 g)
pure vegetable oil   ½-1 qt (½-1 l)

In large heavy fondue pot, heat oil until hot but not boiling. Dice buffalo into 1 inch (2.5 cm) cubes and place on plate or platter. With fondue fork, dip the meat into the hot oil and cook to taste. Serve with the following special sauces:

CURRY SAUCE
Mix:

sour cream   1 part
mayonnaise   1 part
curry powder to taste

APPLE SAUCE
Mix:

apple sauce
cinnamon to taste

PAPRIKA SAUCE
Mix:

horseradish   ⅓ part
sour cream   ⅔ part
paprika to taste

ONION SAUCE
Mix (to taste):

Salad Bowl (Kraft) dressing
onions, finely chopped
bacon bits
parsley, chopped
chives, chopped
onion powder
garlic powder
black pepper
Worcestershire sauce

BUFFALO FONDUE (Continued)

CUMBERLAND SAUCE

raspberry jam	1 part
cranberry sauce	1 part
red wine	$\frac{2}{3}$ part
cinnamon	
corn starch	

Mix jam and cranberry sauce in a small pot and bring to boil. Remove from heat and stir in wine, cinnamon to taste, and corn starch to thicken.

SWEET AND SOUR SAUCE

fresh pineapple, blended	1 part
white vinegar	$\frac{1}{5}$ part
soya sauce	$\frac{1}{5}$ part
ginger	
corn starch	

Over a low heat, mix pineapple, vinegar, and soya sauce together in a small pot. Add ginger to taste and corn starch to thicken.

Louis Lanthier
Chef
THE GRIZZLY HOUSE

"To have only a heavy club between one and a ton and a half of charging buffalo is no adequate protection."

Banff Crag and Canyon, July 17, 1931

FILLETS OF FRESH TROUT
WITH LEMON BUTTER

per serving

fresh trout	1, about 8 oz (225 g)
fresh lemon, juice from	½
whole egg	1
flour	2 tbsp (30 ml)
white wine	½ oz (15 ml)
fresh parsley	sprinkle
butter	1 tbsp (15 ml)
parsley sprigs	
lemon wedges	
vegetable oil	

*Fillet fresh trout. Coat with flour then dip in egg
(lightly beaten). Sauté in oil over a medium heat until
golden brown. Drain oil. Add butter to pan and let melt.
Add juice from lemon, wine and parsley and let boil
for about 1 minute.
Garnish with lemon wedge and parsley. Serve with parsley
sprinkled potato and a vegetable.*

Wesley Hope
Executive Chef
INNS OF BANFF PARK

*"To Preserve Children: Take one large grassy field, one half dozen
children, two or three small dogs, a pinch of brook and some pebbles.
Mix the children and dogs well together and put them in the field,
stirring constantly. Pour the brook over the pebbles and sprinkle
the field with flowers. Spread over all a deep blue sky and bake
in the hot sun. When brown remove and place in a bath to cool."*

Banff Crag and Canyon, June 29, 1928

TOURNEDOS À LA JOSHUA'S

serves four

beef tenderloin pieces	8 4 oz (115 g) pieces
small onion, diced	1
large green pepper, sliced	1
stewed tomatoes, chopped	1 14 oz (398 ml) can
red wine	½ cup (125 ml)
vegetable oil	1 tbsp (15 ml)
garlic clove, crushed	1
Hungarian paprika	1 tsp (5 ml)
prepared mustard	1 tsp (5 ml)
corn starch	1 tsp (5 ml)
beef bouillon cube	1
Worcestershire sauce	
oregano	
salt	
pepper	
white bread	8 slices

*Sauté onions and garlic in oil until onions are transparent.
Add green peppers, stir and sauté for about 2 minutes
over medium heat. Add paprika, stirring quickly, then add
tomatoes and mustard. Add the beef bouillon cube and
season to taste with Worcestershire sauce, oregano, salt and
black pepper. Simmer for 5 minutes. Mix wine and
cornstarch and stir in. Let simmer until thickened.
Croutons: Remove crusts from bread slices and cut bread
into cubes. Fry in hot oil until golden brown on all sides.
Set aside on serving platter.
Season the beef to your taste and fry in hot butter to
your liking. To serve, place meat on croutons and top with
hot sauce.*

*Reinhold Lang
Chef
JOSHUA'S RESTAURANT
& PUB*

*"The old cow is turned loose with a pair of green goggles on,
and as everything looks green to her, hoops, tin cans, chips,
all go the one road, no wonder she is a good milker."*

Banff Crag and Canyon, May 21, 1904

CHICKEN MARQUIS

For chicken:

boneless chicken breast
(per serving) 1
eggs 2
flour

Prepare egg wash by beating eggs in bowl. Lightly flour chicken and then dip completely in the egg wash. In a hot frying pan, sauté the chicken in vegetable oil until golden brown on both sides.

For Chicken Marquis Sauce
six to eight servings

beef stock (or dissolve
cubes of beef base in 5 cups
of boiling water) 40 oz (1⅓ l)
butter 2 oz (60 g)
flour 2 oz (60 g)
white wine 3 oz (80 ml)
medium size onion ½
small tomato 1
salt, pepper, tarragon,
parsley

Slice onion and finely chop tomato and sauté over a medium heat in butter for about 3 minutes. Add flour and stir until smooth. Add a pinch of tarragon and slowly stir in beef stock and white wine. Bring to a boil for about 5 minutes and salt and pepper to taste.
To serve, place chicken on a bed of fluffy white rice and generously cover with sauce. Garnish with a sprig of fresh parsley.

Pierre Marquis
Chef
MELISSA'S MISSTEAK
RESTAURANT & BAR

"Once again the Mounted Police are on the job in Banff and everybody is tickled . . . Banff citizens may now go to bed and snore as hard as they please."

Banff Crag and Canyon, July 28, 1917

ESCALOPE DE VEAU AUX MORILLES
(Veal with Morels)

serves six

morel mushrooms, dried	1 oz (30 g)
unsalted butter	4 tsp (20 ml)
all-purpose flour	¾ cup (185 ml)
onion, chopped	3 tbsp (45 ml)
brandy	2 tbsp (30 ml)
dry white wine	¼ cup (60 ml)
heavy cream	1 cup (250 ml)
fresh lemon juice (or to taste)	2 tsp (30 ml)
salt	
fresh ground black pepper	
veal, from leg or loin	20 oz (560 g)
light olive oil	3 tbsp (45 ml)

*Soak morels in hot water for about 2 hours until soft.
Carefully lift morels from liquid, leaving as much grit as
possible behind. (Discard liquid or strain and reserve
for another use.) Rinse mushrooms in 2 changes of cool
water. Drain and slice lengthwise into very thin strips.
Rinse again, drain well and set aside.
Make a beurre manié by mashing together 1 tsp (5 ml)
butter with 2 tsp (10 ml) flour in a small bowl with
a wooden spoon. When thoroughly blended, set aside.
Melt 3 tsp (15 ml) butter in a heavy medium skillet over a
medium high heat. When foam subsides add onion and sauté,
stirring frequently, until softened. Add morels, sauté and
stir for about 1 minute. Add brandy, shaking pan until
flames are extinguished. Add wine and increase heat to high.
Cook uncovered until liquid is reduced by half.
Add cream to skillet, heat to boiling, and then reduce heat
to medium. Whisk in beurre manié, a little at a time,
until sauce is slightly thickened (so that it coats a metal
spoon). Add lemon juice, salt and pepper to taste.
Cover and keep warm.
Slice veal into about 18 very thin scallops (cut across
the grain and pounded, between 2 sheets of waxed paper,
to ⅛ inch (3 mm) thick) and season on both sides with
salt and pepper to taste. Spread remaining flour on*

ESCALOPE DE VEAU AUX MORILLES
(Continued)

another sheet of waxed paper and dip veal, one scallop at a time, in flour. Shake off excess flour until only a light dusting remains.

Heat a large heavy skillet over a medium high heat until hot enough to evaporate a drop of water on contact. Add about half the oil to the pan, rotate until bottom coated, and heat until smoking. Increase heat to high and add enough scallops to fill pan without crowding. Sear on both sides until browned, then place on warmed serving platter, cover with foil, and keep warm. Repeat until all the veal is sautéed, adding oil to skillet as required.

Reheat sauce, whisking constantly, over a medium heat until heated through. Pour sauce over veal and serve immediately.

Beat Maeder
Chef
POST HOTEL

"There is not much to tell of my trip over Pipestone Pass. It was simply the case of a man starting on a seventy-mile snowshoe trip across the mountains to eat his Christmas dinner with his wife and family, and of getting there and eating the dinner, the pleasure being well worth the trip."

Tom Wilson, pioneer Banff guide,
1909, Canadian Alpine Journal

OMELETTE 'GOURMET'

serves one

whole eggs	3
crab meat	1 oz (30 g)
blue cheese, grated	½ oz (15 g)
fresh mushrooms	½ oz (15 g)
green onions	½ oz (15 g)
clarified butter	
salt	
black pepper	

*Chop green onions. Slice mushrooms and sauté
in a small skillet.
Crack eggs and place in bowl with salt and pepper and
whip until frothy. Put clarified butter in an omelette pan
over medium heat and pour in eggs. When eggs are firm,
place crab meat, blue cheese, mushrooms and green onions
on one side and fold eggs over to seal. Cook until cheese
melts and serve with salt and pepper to taste.*

*C. Allan Winder
Executive Chef
RIMROCK INN*

*"A bachelor is a man who looks before he leaps and then
doesn't leap."*

Banff Crag and Canyon, June 15, 1928

CHICKEN MARYLAND

serves four

boneless chicken breasts	**4**
white wine	**1 cup (250 ml)**
flour	
eggs	**4**
milk	**¼ cup (60 ml)**
honey	**1 cup (250 ml)**
orange juice, fresh squeezed	**½ cup (125 ml)**
brandy	**½ cup (125 ml)**
cornstarch	**4 tsp (20 ml)**
water	
fresh whole banana	**1**

*Soak chicken breasts in wine for at least 2 hours. Dip in
flour, then eggs (lightly beaten). Pan fry until golden brown.
Combine honey, orange juice and brandy in double boiler
and bring to a gentle boil. Thicken with a mixture of
cornstarch and water if required.
To serve, place chicken breasts on bed of fluffy white rice,
cover with sauce and garnish with banana slices.*

*SUNSHINE VILLAGE SKI
AND SUMMER RESORT*

*"Dress your duck and allow a slow cook to walk through a hot
kitchen with it."*

*comment on cooking duck rare
1924, Elon Jessup in 'Camp Grub'*

FILET DE VEAU ZURICHOISE
(Veal with Mushroom Sauce)

serves six

veal tenderloin	27 oz (750 g)
fresh mushrooms	16 oz (450 g)
onion	1
dry white wine	1 cup (250 ml)
unsalted butter	8 oz (225 g)
flour	12 oz (340 g)
heavy cream	4 oz (115 g)
lemon	1
salt	
pepper	
Worcestershire sauce	

Finely dice onions and sauté with butter in an enameled or stainless steel skillet. Wash and slice mushrooms and add to onions. Cook over a medium high heat, stirring, until mushrooms are golden. Add wine, salt, pepper, Worcestershire sauce and juice from lemon and bring to a boil for 2 to 3 minutes; then separate mushrooms from the sauce and set aside. Thicken sauce by adding lumps of beurre manié — made by kneading together tablespoon sized lumps of flour and butter. Stir in heavy cream, add the mushrooms again and season to taste.
Slice the veal into 24 slices, spice to taste and roll in flour.
In a large frying pan sauté in vegetable oil until done.
Arrange veal on plate, top with sauce, garnish with a rosette of whipping cream and sprinkle with chopped parsley.
Serve with buttered noodles.

Hermann Zehnder
Chef
TICINO SWISS-ITALIAN
RESTAURANT

"A daring robbery . . . while Fred was away . . . he left hanging . . . a good sized leg of lamb that would make the teeth of an epicurean chatter . . . a couple of coyotes got scent of the layout . . . Fred returned . . . and discovered his loss . . . The last heard of him that night he was busy saying the Lord's prayer in the United States language."

Banff Crag and Canyon, May 21, 1904

FETTUCINE ALFREDO

serves four

egg noodles, narrow style	12 oz (340 g)
medium tomato	1
medium green pepper	1
ham, pre-cooked	3 oz (85 g)
fresh mushrooms	3 oz (85 g)
onion	½
egg yolks	4
heavy cream	12 oz (340 ml)
Parmesan cheese, grated	2-2½ oz (50-70 g)
salt	
white pepper	
nutmeg	
parsley flakes	
fresh parsley	

*Cut tomato, green pepper, ham and mushrooms into ⅛ inch
(3 mm) cubes (brunoise style) and sauté in large frying pan,
teflon if possible. Beat egg yolks and cream together. Stir
cheese, then cream mixture into pan. Season to taste.
Cook noodles 'al dente' then strain. While still hot add
to pan. Mix gently until all ingredients are well distributed.
Garnish with parsley flakes, a tomato slice, a twig of
fresh parsley and serve.*

Hermann Zehnder
Chef
TICINO SWISS-ITALIAN
RESTAURANT

*"The writer who wrote . . . that the Canadian Rockies have the
grandeur and beauty of the Alps, but lack the romance and poetry,
has a long guess coming . . . Regarding romance and poetry, it
largely depends on the number of summer girls around."*

Banff Crag and Canyon, August 2, 1912

SEAFOOD BURRITOS

for one serving

8 inch (20 cm) flour tortillas	2
snow crab meat	½ cup (125 ml)
pre-cooked small shrimp	½ cup (125 ml)
onion, diced	¼ cup (60 ml)
canned green chilies, diced	1 tbsp (15 ml)
enchilada sauce, red or green homemade or commercial	2 oz (60 g)
jack or brick cheese, grated	¼ cup (60 ml)
tomato, diced	¼ cup (60 ml)
sour cream	1 oz (30 g)
basil leaves, crushed	
aromatic seasoning salt	
shredded lettuce	
lemon wedges	
parsley sprig	

Over medium heat, sauté onion and chilies in butter or margarine until onions are transparent. Stir in crab and shrimp. Add basil and seasoning salt to taste. Cook 3 to 4 minutes until seafood is hot but not overdone. Remove from heat.
Place tortillas on large plate and place proportionate row of seafood mixture across the centre of each. Top each row with diced tomato and sour cream. Roll tortillas around mixture and centre on plate. Cover with enchilada sauce and grated cheese.
Preheat oven to 450°F (230°C) and bake burritos for 10 to 15 minutes until cheese is melted and enchilada sauce is bubbling. Garnish with shredded lettuce, lemon wedges and parsley sprig. Serve with Spanish rice and refried beans.

Genny Bellah &
Michael Roberge
Chefs
THE YARD

Facing Page: Morning at Moraine Lake
Douglas Leighton Photograph

SOUPS
& SALADS

'A light lunch in the Rockies',
at Lake O'Hara, 1897
Vaux Family Photograph

CONTENTS

"Tuesday night's frost did a good deal of damage to the gardens in the village and the Chinaman who supplies so many houses with fresh vegetables is complaining that "belly cold fleese um evlyting"."

Banff Crag and Canyon, September 7, 1912

BALKAN CAESAR SALAD

serves two

romaine lettuce	1 medium head
croutons	½ cup (125 ml)
egg yolk	1
Parmesan cheese, grated	4 tbsp (60 ml)
garlic	2 cloves
anchovies	3
olive oil	5 tbsp (75 ml)
red wine vinegar	1 tbsp (15 ml)
dry hot mustard	⅛ tsp (½ ml)
Worcestershire sauce	8 drops
Tabasco sauce	2 drops
lemon	½
salt	
black pepper	

*Put garlic cloves in a wooden bowl and crush well.
Thoroughly mash anchovies and add them. Add mustard,
egg yolk and juice from lemon. Mix well using two forks.
Add vinegar, oil, Worcestershire sauce, Tabasco sauce,
and salt and pepper to taste. Mix well; the more thoroughly,
the better. Wash and dry lettuce. Break up lettuce, put in
bowl and toss very well. Sprinkle with Parmesan cheese,
top with croutons and serve.*

Jason Karlos
Chef
BALKAN VILLAGE
RESTAURANT

*"You can't enjoy the most entrancing view or even be sociable with
your fellow men if your stomach is full of say — burnt beans."*

*Harold Pripps, quoted by
Elon Jessup in 'Camp Grub', 1924*

CHICKEN SALAD BORNEO

serves four

medium stewing chicken	1
pineapple chunks, drained	1 can, 14 oz (398 ml)
mayonnaise	½ cup (125 ml)
celery stalk, finely diced	1
green onions, finely diced	2
curry powder	2 tbsp (30 ml)
mango chutney	¼ cup (60 ml)
salt	
pepper	
romaine lettuce	
orange slices	
chopped hazelnuts	

In a large pot, boil chicken until meat comes away from the bones with a fork. Remove chicken, clean meat from bones, and roughly chop. Reserve the stock for soup.
In a mixing bowl, mix chicken chunks thoroughly with pineapple chunks, mayonnaise, celery, onion, curry powder, chutney, and salt and pepper to taste. Add more mayonnaise if too dry.
Serve on a bed of romaine lettuce and garnish with orange slices and chopped hazelnuts.

Laura Buckley
Chef
BANFF ROCKY
MOUNTAIN RESORT

"Mr. Helm . . . became hopelessly lost . . . when . . . found . . . he was, or seemed to be partly delirious, keeping up a strange conversation about a lot of mermaids he saw . . . through a large hole in a rock . . . We all know Mr. Helm is of sound mind . . . (and) it was some days before . . . the mystery was cleared . . . eight ladies who were bathing in the Cave, complained of a nasty, bold man watching them sporting in the waters of life.

Mr. Helm was never a confirmed bachelor . . . and now carries a set of opera glasses and swears that next time he will not be fooled easily."

Banff Crag and Canyon, July 26, 1902

CHILLED CUCUMBER AND APPLE SOUP

serves 6

cucumbers, peeled, seeded and diced	18 oz (500 g)
apples, peeled, cored and diced	9 oz (250 g)
garlic, crushed	½ clove
white vinegar	1 tbsp (15 ml)
olive oil	1 tbsp (15 ml)
chicken stock, strong	3 tbsp (45 ml)
fresh mint	6 leaves
lemon, juice from	½
plain yogurt	4 oz (115 g)
dill, chopped	½ tsp (2 ml)
fresh cream	7 oz (200 ml)

*Place all ingredients, except cream, in blender or
food processor and blend to fine purée.
Whip fresh cream and fold into mixture. Pour into
pre-cooled soup cups and refrigerate.
To garnish, pipe rosette of whipped cream and sprinkle
chives or chopped dill on top.*

*Martin Luthi
Executive Chef
BANFF SPRINGS HOTEL*

*"But, as fate would have it, someone had dropped a pat of butter on
one of the two steps which lead into the room and, as happens once
in every waiter's life, . . . (Oscar) and the fish went down
together. To the not-so-dulcet sound of some not-so-polite snickers,
Oscar pieced the fish together and proceeded to Reynold's table
where he served the meal as best he could with one arm — the other
had been broken in the fall!"*

*an episode in the life of the
extraordinarily dedicated 1920's waiter
Oscar, by Bart Robinson, in his
Banff Springs — The Story of a Hotel;
Summerthought, Ltd., Banff, 1973*

BELGIUM ENDIVE WITH MANDARINE DRESSING

serves 6

Belgium endive heads	3
plain yogurt	9 oz (250 g)
mandarine sections, fresh or canned, chopped	3½ oz (100 g)
dry mustard	¼ tsp (1 ml)
lemon, juice from	½
orange, juice from	1
whipping cream	¾ cup (185 ml)
salt	dash
black ground pepper	dash

Remove the large leaves carefully from each head, without breaking them. Cut the remaining small leaves in julienne (fine) strips. In separate containers, soak the large leaves and the julienne strips in cold salted water for 20 minutes. Drain and dry.
To prepare the dressing put yogurt, lemon and orange juice, dry mustard, mandarine sections and seasonings in a bowl and mix well with a whisk. Whip cream and fold into yogurt mixture.
Divide the dressing into 6 burgundy or large wine glasses and set the endive leaves along the rim into the dressing. Place the julienne strips in the centre.
It is perfectly proper to eat this salad with your hands.

Martin Luthi
Executive Chef
BANFF SPRINGS HOTEL

"Balloon jumping is the newest sport in England. You attach a small balloon to yourself and it makes you so buoyant that you can jump over barns, haystacks, and trees with ease."

Banff Crag and Canyon, May 8, 1925

BANFF SPRINGS SALAD

Take a large size ripe tomato, empty it and prepare a tuna fish salad with chopped celery, parsley and egg. Mix it with a little mayonnaise and season to taste. Refill the tomato with the salad, dress on lettuce, decorate it with asparagus tips, sliced beets and watercress, then serve with thousand island dressing.

STUFFED TOMATO CANADIENNE

Take a good size ripe tomato, empty it and prepare a stuffing with the following ingredients:
Sausage meat or cooked beef or veal, the tomato pulp with seeds removed, spring onions and parsley chopped together, mix with a little boiled rice and tomato catsup, well season the mixture and refill the tomato. Over it spread bread crumbs and a little butter, then bake. Serve with tomato sauce.

> *M. Henri Odiau*
> *Chef*
> ***BANFF SPRINGS HOTEL***
> *reprinted from*
> ***Banff Crag and Canyon,***
> ***August 8, 1930***

"A cow is a female quadruped with an alto voice and a countenance in which there is no guile. She collaborates with the pump in the production of a liquid called milk, provides filler for hash, and at last, is skinned by those she has benefited, as mortals commonly are."

Banff Crag and Canyon, June 15, 1928

BUMPER'S BEEF BARLEY SOUP

makes 15 cups

beef soup base	4 oz (115 g)
water	8 cups (2 l)
barley	1 cup (250 ml)
whole tomatoes, hand crushed	2 cups (500 ml)
crushed tomatoes	1 cup (250 ml)
tomato juice	½ cup (125 ml)
onion, diced to ½ inch (1 cm)	1 cup (250 ml)
celery, diced to ½ inch (1 cm)	1 cup (250 ml)
carrots, diced to ½ inch (1 cm)	1 cup (250 ml)
turnip, diced to ½ inch (1 cm)	1 cup (250 ml)
beef, cut in 1 inch (2½ cm) cubes and pre-cooked	8 oz (225 g)
thyme	¼ tsp (1 ml)
oregano	¼ tsp (1 ml)
garlic powder	¼ tsp (1 ml)
basil	¼ tsp (1 ml)
Worcestershire sauce	1 tsp (5 ml)
bay leaf	1

Bring water to a boil in a 4 qt (4 l) pot and add the beef soup base. Warm barley with warm water to remove excess starch. Strain and add to pot. When barley is cooked about half through, add tomatoes, crushed tomatoes and tomato juice. Then add the diced vegetables, simmering on low heat until vegetables are about half cooked. Add beef cubes and spices and continue simmering until vegetables are well cooked. Remove bay leaf and serve immediately. This soup can also be cooled and reheated.

BUMPER'S
THE BEEF HOUSE

"Banff, North-West Territory — 'A Medicinal Watering Place and Pleasure Resort' "

from government advertisement, Banff Crag and Canyon, 1901

ALMOND SOUP

serves six to eight

almonds, sliced and blanched	2 cups (500 ml)
chicken broth	4 cups (1 l)
additional chicken broth or water	3 cups (750 ml)
medium onion, diced	1
lemon	1
peppercorns	a few
cardamom pods, seeds from	2 or 3
caraway seeds	½ tsp (2 ml)
salt	pinch
heavy cream	1 cup (250 ml)
long grain white converted rice	½ cup (125 ml)
currants	⅓ cup (85 ml)

Lightly toast almonds on baking sheet in oven. Combine almonds with 1 qt (1 l) of chicken broth in food processor or blender. Pour into a heavy saucepan and heat.
Sauté onions in butter and add to almond broth. Add salt, seeds, peppercorns and zest (grated peel) from lemon and let simmer for 1 hour.
Press almond broth mixture through sieve and set liquid aside to simmer in second pot. Return pulp to saucepan, add 3 cups of chicken broth or water and let simmer for 1 hour. Sieve again and add liquid to first batch. Discard pulp.
Season almond broth to taste and add cream. Let simmer. About ½ hour before serving add rice to broth; about 15 minutes before serving add currants. To serve, garnish with dark croutons or toasted almond flakes.

Lynne Grillmair
Chef
Bugaboo Lodge
CANADIAN MOUNTAIN HOLIDAYS

"Do you want to BORROW MONEY . . . and pay 5 per cent interest . . . ?"

advertisement, Banff Crag and Canyon, August 2, 1912

CHAWAN MUSHI
(Japanese Custard Soup)

serves six to eight

spinach leaves, deveined and chopped	10
raw shrimp, peeled and deveined	8
or	
slivers of raw chicken breast	
or	
pieces of crabmeat	
fresh raw mushrooms, sliced	½ cup (125 ml)
water chestnuts	8
or	
slices of peeled broccoli stem	
dry sherry	¼ cup (60 ml)
eggs	4
chicken stock	3 cups (750 ml)
sugar	1 tsp (5 ml)
soya sauce	1 tbsp (15 ml)

Place spinach leaves, shrimp, mushrooms and water chestnuts in the bottoms of 6 to 8 custard cups (or coffee mugs) and add sherry to each. Slightly beat the eggs, then beat the eggs, chicken stock, sugar and soya sauce together. Divide and pour into custard cups.
Set filled custard cups on a rack in a deep pan and semi-submerge with water. Cover and bring to a slow boil over medium heat. Then reduce heat and let cook for about 10 to 15 minutes or until custard sets (when an inserted knife will come out clean).

Lynne Grillmair
Chef
Bugaboo Lodge
CANADIAN MOUNTAIN HOLIDAYS

"A wise man once said: 'Every one who has health and strength and is able to kick about the things that don't suit them ought to be satisfied.'"

Banff Crag and Canyon, August 29, 1903

VINEGARETTE OF LEEKS

serves four

leeks	**4**
vegetable oil	**½ cup (125 ml)**
red wine vinegar	**2 tbsp (30 ml)**
hot mustard	**½ tsp (2 ml)**
salt	
black pepper	

*Remove tough outside leaves from leeks and discard.
Wash and drain well. Split leeks in half lengthwise and
slice into ⅛ inch (3 mm) strips. Steam for 20 to 30 minutes
until tender, then drain and let cool.
Prepare light dressing by mixing together oil, vinegar,
hot mustard and salt and pepper to taste. Mix dressing
thoroughly with leeks. Let stand in refrigerator for
1 to 2 hours before serving.*

BUTTER LETTUCE 'MIMOSA'

serves four

*Select the tender leaves from one large head of butter
lettuce and wash well. Garnish with fresh sliced mushrooms,
tomato wedges and chopped green peppers. Sprinkle
chopped hard boiled egg on top and serve with spicy
vinegarette (above).*

*Jaroslav Nydr
Executive Chef*
CHATEAU LAKE LOUISE

*"Carl Rungius, the great animal painter of New York, was a guest
this week at the King Edward. He then went north with Jimmy
Simpson as guide. Jimmy will sure lead him into green pastures
and beside still waters."*

Banff Crag and Canyon, August 4, 1917

MOUNTAINEER'S SALAD

serves one to two

Cervelle, Bratwurst or veal sausage	4 oz (115 g)
Swiss Casino cheese	4 oz (115 g)
green pepper	1 oz (30 g)
onions	1 oz (30 g)
tomato	1 oz (30 g)
cucumber	1 oz (30 g)
hot mustard	½ oz (15 ml)
olive oil	½ oz (15 ml)
lemon juice	½ oz (15 ml)
salt	
pepper	
thyme	
lettuce leaf	
tomato wedges	
fresh parsley	

In a small bowl mix mustard, olive oil, lemon juice, and salt, pepper and thyme to taste.
Dice sausage, cheese and vegetables into ¼ inch (6 mm) cubes and place in a bowl. Add liquids from other bowl and stir to distribute ingredients thoroughly.
Serve on lettuce leaf garnished with tomato wedges and parsley.

THE GRIZZLY HOUSE

"Children in Japan now sit upon chairs instead of squatting . . .
This is being done as an attempt to make their legs grow longer."

Banff Crag and Canyon, Aug. 31, 1912

QUESO SOPAS
(Cheese Soup)

serves six to eight

all purpose flour	1 cup (250 ml)
butter	4 oz (115 g)
green peppers, diced	¼ cup (60 ml)
onions, diced	¼ cup (60 ml)
white pepper	1 tsp (5 ml)
garlic powder	1 tsp (5 ml)
brick cheese, grated	9 oz (250 g)
Monterey jack cheese, grated	9 oz (250 g)
chicken broth	3½ cups (850 ml)
cheddar cheese, grated	
milk	

Heat broth. Combine butter, vegetables and spices in a saucepan over high heat and cook until butter is completely melted and vegetables are done. Add flour to butter-vegetable mixture and whisk rapidly until smooth and all butter is absorbed. Add heated broth and stir rapidly until butter-flour mixture dissolves. Let simmer on medium high heat until thickened. Add grated cheese and stir in until smooth. Thin to desired consistency with milk. To serve, top with grated cheddar cheese and broil in oven until nicely browned.

MAGPIE & STUMP

"Sing a song of wildcat, raise a little scare, one on Tunnel Mountain, William saw it there. Four boys hunted pussy, Thursday of this week, but they couldn't find her, and she's still to seek."

Banff Crag and Canyon, May 19, 1906

GUACAMOLE DIP

serves six to eight

ripe avacados	8
onions, diced	½ cup (125 ml)
dried tomatoes	½ cup (125 ml)
salsa*	2 cups (500 ml)
garlic powder	2 tsp (10 ml)
lemon juice	¼ cup (60 ml)
seasoning salt	2 tsp (10 ml)

Peel and mash avacados. Add vegetables, salsa, spices and lemon juice and mix thoroughly. Cool in refrigerator and serve.
Guacamole does not keep well and is best prepared in small amounts and served 2 to 4 hours after preparation.

(* See Salsa recipe, page 94.)

MAGPIE & STUMP

"It is not the high cost of living that keeps young people from marriage these days, but the cost of high living; when a young man calls on a young lady now . . . he has to take her out — and feed her!"

Banff Crag and Canyon, Mar. 29, 1928

MELISSA'S HOMEMADE
VEGETABLE SOUP

serves eight

carrots, sliced	**2 cups (500 ml)**
onions, sliced and chopped	**1½ cups (375 ml)**
potatoes, coarsely chopped	**2 cups (500 ml)**
celery, sliced	**1½ cups (375 ml)**
green cabbage, chopped	**2½ cups (625 ml)**
green pepper, chopped	**½ cup (125 ml)**
lentils	**½ cup (125 ml)**
chicken soup base	**2 oz (60 g)**
beef soup base	**1 oz (30 g)**
onion soup base	**1 oz (30 g)**
crushed tomatoes, canned	**20 oz (570 ml)**
sliced mushrooms, canned	**14 oz (398 ml)**
salt (or to taste)	**1¼ oz (35 g)**
Italian spice (or to taste)	**¾ oz (22 g)**
water	**20 cups (5 l)**

*In a large pot, bring water to a boil. Add the carrots and
lentils and let boil for 10 minutes. Then add the rest of the
vegetables (except for the potatoes), the soup bases and*   ·
*spices. Let boil for 10 minutes then add the potatoes,
crushed tomatoes, and mushrooms (and black pepper to taste
if desired). Simmer for 20 minutes or until the potatoes
are cooked through.*

*MELISSA'S MISSTEAK
RESTAURANT & BAR*

*". . . (the old mountain goat) was not cut down in the bloom of his
youth; for though 'K' pounded his steaks to jelly on the stones,
and boiled and simmered his legs for hours, he failed to be
'chewable' let alone digestable . . . and no one of that party ever
again sighed for goat."*

*Mary T.S. Schaffer, 1911,
in 'Old Indian Trails of the
Canadian Rockies'*

MULLIGATAWNY SOUP

serves ten

beef	1½ lbs (675 g)
medium carrots	4
zucchini	3
green pepper	2
celery stalks	10
beef stock	2½ qts (2½ l)
butter	5 oz (140 g)
flour	5 oz (140 g)
stewed tomatoes, canned	8 oz (225 g)
bay leaves	2
crushed garlic	3 tbsp (45 ml)
curry powder	4 tsp (20 ml)
Worcestershire sauce	1 oz (30 ml)

*Dice vegetables and beef into ½ inch (1 cm) cubes.
Sauté vegetables gently for 4-5 minutes and sauté
beef lightly.
Put beef stock in large pot and bring to boil.
Over low heat, melt butter in a skillet and add flour,
stirring steadily, until this 'roux' has a sandy consistency.
Add the roux to the boiling beef stock and stir in well.
Then add the sautéed vegetables and beef, bay leaves, garlic
and seasonings to taste. Let simmer for 45 minutes,
remove bay leaves and serve.*

*Stan Staz
Chef
THE MOUNTAIN
GREENERY RESTAURANT
AND DANCE CLUB*

*Facing Page: Mule Deer Fawn in Mountain Meadow
Douglas Leighton Photograph*

BREAKFASTS
& DESSERTS

'Enjoy!',
Baker with display, 1923
Byron Harmon Photograph

CONTENTS

"The good old Alberta dining room . . . will on September 3, close its doors . . . after that date there will be a number of hungry boarders, who frequently eat an awful lot and seldom very little, looking around for a new grub pile."

Banff Crag and Canyon, August 18, 1917

MOUNTAIN OMELETTE

serves six

eggs	12
green peppers	2
large onion	1
fresh mushrooms	8 oz (225 g)
smoked ham	14 oz (400 g)
cheddar cheese, grated	6 oz (170 g)
mozzarella cheese, grated	6 oz (170 g)
butter	4 oz (115 g)
half-and-half or 10% cream	1 pint (½ l)

Wash and slice mushrooms. Dice green peppers, onion, and ham into ⅛ inch (3 mm) squares. Over a low heat, melt half the butter in a large skillet and sauté the above ingredients for about 4 minutes.
In a bowl, combine eggs and cream and whip until frothy. Melt remaining butter in omelette pan. For each serving, pour ⅙ of the egg mixture into the pan (over a medium heat) and let cook for about 3 minutes. Then place ⅙ of grated cheese and diced ingredients on one side of eggs and fold over to seal. Cook about 2 more minutes to allow cheese to melt.

Rob Logan
Chef
THE MOUNTAIN
GREENERY RESTAURANT
AND DANCE CLUB

"Good old days on the trail . . . When the coffee pot upset . . . and the sugar and salt got wet and sometimes the beans went sour and the bacon musty and the wind blew smoke in your eyes . . . and the mosquitoes almost crowded you out . . . how I wish I could live them all over again!"

Tom Wilson, pioneer Banff guide, reminiscing in the Banff Crag and Canyon, May 1, 1925

HUEVOS RANCHEROS

serves one

corn tortillas	2 - 6 inch (15 cm)
eggs	2
home made or commercial salsa	2 oz (60 g)
medium cheddar cheese, grated	½ cup (125 ml)
jack cheese, grated	½ cup (125 ml)
orange slice	
tomato slice	
fresh parsley	

*In a skillet or deep fryer, slightly blanch tortillas in
vegetable oil. They should be kept flexible. Drain excess oil
from them and pat dry with a paper towel. Place tortillas
side by side on a plate and set aside.
Either fry or scramble the eggs. Place them on top of
tortillas and cover with salsa. If you wish, make this dish
more zesty with additional salsa or seasoning to taste.
Top eggs, sauce and tortillas with grated cheeses and bake
or broil until cheese is melted.
(Do not brown cheese as this will overcook the eggs.)
Garnish with orange, tomato and parsley. Serve with toast
and hash brown potatoes.
(See Salsa recipe, page 94)*

*Genny Bellah and
Michael Roberge
Chefs
THE YARD*

*"J. Raby lost one of his hens last Sunday, when a dog with a taste
from Alabama helped itself. It afterwards made a return trip but
Jim was waiting with a lasso and caught the blighter. The sad part
about it is the fact that it was the only hen that knew anything
about eggs."*

Banff Crag and Canyon, Mar. 24, 1928

YOGURT WITH HONEY AND WALNUTS

serves two

plain yogurt	1 cup (250 ml)
honey	3 tbsp (45 ml)
chopped walnuts	1 tbsp (15 ml)

*Divide yogurt and place in 2 small dessert dishes.
Top with honey, sprinkle with walnuts and serve.*

Jason Karlos
Chef
BALKAN VILLAGE
RESTAURANT

PECAN PIE

makes two 9 inch (23 cm) pies

corn syrup	1 cup (250 ml)
brown sugar	1 cup (250 ml)
eggs	3
butter	⅓ cup (80 ml)
molasses	4 tbsp (60 ml)
bourbon	6 tbsp (90 ml)
vanilla	1 tsp (5 ml)
salt	⅓ tsp (1½ ml)
pecan halves	1 cup (250 ml)

*Mix the corn syrup and brown sugar together. Beat the
eggs slightly. Melt the butter and beat into syrup mixture
with eggs, molasses, bourbon, vanilla and salt.
Divide pecans and place in two 9 inch (23 cm) pie pans
lined with pastry and pour in pie filling mixture. Bake at
400°F (200°C) for about 45 minutes.*

BANFF PARK LODGE

LEMON LOAF

makes four 3″ X 3″ x 9″ (8 cm x 8 cm x 23 cm) loaves

butter	1 lb (450 g)
sugar	4½ cups (1 l + 60 ml)
eggs	8
lemons	4
flour	6 cups (1½ l)
salt	1 tsp (5 ml)
baking powder	4 tsp (20 ml)
milk	2 cups (500 ml)

*Grate zest (peel) from lemons. Cream the butter,
add 4 cups (1 l) sugar and mix well. Beat in the eggs and
lemon zest. Mix flour with baking powder and salt.
Alternately, mix in flour and milk, ¹/₃ at a time.
Pour into 3 greased and floured loaf pans.
Bake in a 350°F (180°C) oven for about 40 minutes
or until done.
About ³/₄ through baking, glaze with a mixture of the juice
from the lemons and the remaining 12 tsp (60 ml) of sugar.
To store, wrap well in plastic and refrigerate.*

BANFF PARK LODGE

*"A young girl . . . (at) dinner was observed to eat her pie first. When
asked why, she replied: 'Well, if there's anything left, it won't be the
pie . . .'"*

Banff Crag and Canyon, July 15, 1901

CARAMEL PEARS

serves six

fresh ripe pears	6 medium
white sugar	7 oz (200 g)
white wine	2⅓ cups (600 ml)
lemon, juice from	1
egg yolks	4
whipping cream	1 cup (250 ml)
raisins	7 oz (200 g)
dark rum	1⅔ oz (50 ml)

*Soak raisins in rum for 30 minutes. Peel pears, leaving stem
in place. Core pears from bottom, using melon scoop.
Fill cavity with soaked raisins.
Use a small saucepan deep enough to submerge ⅔ of each
pear in liquid. Put sugar in saucepan and add 4 tbsp
(60 ml) of water and cook to caramel state. Add white wine
slowly and carefully as pan will be extremely hot.
Add lemon juice and simmer until all sugar is dissolved.
Add pears, cover and poach until tender. Remove pears
carefully and place into serving dish. Reduce liquid to
about ⅔ cup (160 ml) and add cream. Heat to about 106°F
(60°C), use a candy thermometer. In a blender, whip egg
yolks then slowly add liquid from pan. Blend well. If sauce
is too thin, place on stove and heat while stirring until
thickened. (Do not boil.)
Pour sauce over pears.*

*Martin Luthi
Executive Chef
BANFF SPRINGS HOTEL*

" "I told my wife that if she bobbed her hair I would leave her."

"But she bobbed it; and you're still living with her?"

"You bet I am. I'll show her that she can't bluff me." "

Banff Crag and Canyon, May 1, 1925

LE GATEAU POIRE WILLIAM
(Pear William Cake)

makes one 9 inch (23 cm cake)

whole eggs	4
egg yolks	2
sugar	4½ oz (125 g)
flour	3½ oz (100 g)
cornstarch	2 oz (60 g)
cocoa powder	½ oz (15 g)
Pear William brandy	2 oz (60 ml)
pears, cooked and halved	4
dark chocolate	5½ oz (160 g)
water	3 oz (85 ml)
gelatine	½ oz (15 g)
whipping cream	16 oz (500 ml)
butter	

Combine the eggs, egg yolks and sugar in a large metal mixing bowl. Heat slightly (place mixing bowl in pan of heated water) and beat mixture until smooth and thick. Mix the flour, cocoa, and cornstarch together; then stir gently into egg mixture. Pour in to a buttered cake form and bake in a pre-heated 375°F (190°C) oven for 20 minutes or until done.
Remove cake from oven, let settle for 10 minutes, and then remove from form and let cool completely.
Put cake back in form and sprinkle with brandy.
Arrange pears on top of the cake and cover with the following cream: dissolve the gelatine in the heated water. Melt the chocolate and mix in. Whip the cream and fold in. Pour on top of cake in form and let sit until cream has thickened.

Gerhard Frey
Chef
LE BEAUJOLAIS

" 'What is life?' asked the wise looking man in spectacles.
'Two weeks in Banff', said the Calgary girl, 'that's life for me.' "

Banff Crag and Canyon, August 20, 1904

STRAWBERRY BAVARIAN

serves eight

egg yolks	3
sugar	⅓ cup (75 ml)
milk	1½ cup (375 ml)
gelatine	2 tbsp (30 ml)
orange juice, chilled	¼ cup (60 ml)
vanilla	1 tsp (5 ml)
puréed strawberries, or frozen strawberries, thawed and drained	1 cup (250 ml)
strawberries, diced or frozen, thawed and drained	½ cup (125 ml)
nectarines, fresh and diced	½ cup (125 ml)
pineapple, freshly cooked and diced	½ cup (125 ml)
Kirsch	2 tbsp (30 ml)
whipping cream	½ cup (125 ml)

Beat together egg yolks and sugar. Scald milk and pour in slowly, stirring constantly. Return to stove and cook over low heat until mixture coats a metal spoon. (Do not boil.) Remove from heat and stir in gelatine (pre-mixed) and orange juice mixture and vanilla. Put saucepan in pan of ice water to cool. Stir.
In a small bowl, soak the diced fruit in Kirsch. When custard cools to thicken enough to form a mound on a spoon, stir in puréed strawberries. Then stir in the soaked fruit and Kirsch and juice. Whip the whipping cream and fold in. Spoon into 8 tall parfait glasses, garnish with strawberries or sliced fruit and chill well before serving.

Lynne Grillmair
Chef
Bugaboo Lodge
CANADIAN MOUNTAIN HOLIDAYS

"If you don't know why a strawberry short-cake is so called, look for the strawberries."

Banff Crag and Canyon, June 17, 1901

ZUCCHINI BREAD

brown sugar	1 cup (250 ml)
eggs	2
vegetable oil	1 cup (250 ml)
vanilla	1 tsp (5 ml)
zucchini, grated	1½ cups (375 ml)
flour	2 cups (500 ml)
salt	½ tsp (2 ml)
baking soda	½ tsp (2 ml)
baking powder	1 tsp (5 ml)
cinnamon	4 tsp (20 ml)

Beat eggs and sugar together until creamy. Slowly stir in vegetable oil and then zucchini and vanilla. In a separate bowl, sift together flour, salt, baking soda, baking powder, and cinnamon; then add to the zucchini mixture and stir in gently (be careful not to over mix). Pour into greased loaf pan(s) and bake at 350°F (180°C) for about one hour or until test skewer comes out clean from centre.
Slice and serve with Orange Sauce (page 91).

Kathleen Wilson
Pastry Chef
CHATEAU LAKE LOUISE

". . . to give the trail-breakers a welcome, a bright idea popped into my head. 'They shall have a boiled pudding.' I made the pudding and we all tasted it and it was a good pudding, that is if it had been intended for a cannon-ball . . . our campsite may fade, our trip forgotten, but that pudding ought to be there when the next explorers go through."

Mary T.S. Schaffer, 1911, in
'Old Indian Trails of the Canadian Rockies'

WHITE CHOCOLATE MOUSSE

serves six

30% whipping cream	1 cup (250 ml)
quality white chocolate	5½ oz (150 g)
white sugar	1½ oz (40 g)
unsalted butter	3½ oz (100 g)
egg whites	9
egg yolks	3
whiskey (rye or bourbon)	½ oz (15 ml)

In separate bowls, beat egg yolks with sugar until white and smooth and whip cream, while gradually adding whiskey, until stiff. Melt the chocolate and butter together in a double broiler over a low heat. Then whip egg whites until stiff in a third bowl.
Mix the egg yolk and sugar mixture into the melted chocolate and butter. Then gently fold in to this the whipped egg whites and cream. Pour mixture into 6 chilled glasses and refrigerate for at least 6 hours before serving.

Patrice Durandeau and
John Mayes
Chefs
DEER LODGE

"Banff is a playground set midst wondrous beauty, but Lake Louise is Beauty's Shrine . . . the Mona Lisa of the Mountains."

Banff Crag and Canyon, June 15, 1928

RUM CHOCOLATE MOUSSE

serves twenty

whipping cream	1½ qts (1½ l)
white sugar	6 oz (170 g)
dark rum	3½ oz (100 ml)
Toblerone Swiss chocolate	9 oz (250 g)
eggs	7
semi-sweet Baker's chocolate, grated	

*In a saucepan, over a low heat, melt chocolate and stir in
sugar and rum. Let cool in refrigerator for at least 1 hour.
In a medium bowl, whip whites from eggs and then add the
cold base, mixing gently.
In a large bowl, whip the whipping cream and then add the
other base, mixing gently.
Put mixture into 20 champagne glasses, top with
whipped cream and grated baker's chocolate, and chill for
at least 2 hours before serving.*

Louis Lanthier
Chef
THE GRIZZLY HOUSE

*"The Arctic Ice Company . . . arrived last week and are busily . . .
(cutting) ice from the Bow River. The ice, like nearly everything else
in Banff, is of excellent quality, and is 26 inches in thickness."*

Banff Crag and Canyon, Mar. 11, 1901

BITTER CHOCOLATE ICE CREAM

makes about one gallon (4½ l)

Baker's unsweetened chocolate	3-8 oz (225 g) boxes
whipping cream	2 qts (2¼ l)
half and half cream	2 qts (2¼ l)
Espresso coffee	2 cups (500 ml)
egg yolks, large	6
sugar	5-6 cups (1¼-1½ l)
sliced almonds	

Over a low heat, melt chocolate in a double boiler. Stir in coffee with a wooden spoon. Add whipping cream one part at a time and gently fold in after each addition. Stir in sugar, half and half cream and (beaten) egg yolks. Thoroughly blend all ingredients together. Remove from heat and allow 2 hours to cool. Put in ice cream machine and freeze churn until ready. Serve with sliced almonds.

Wesley Hope
Executive Chef
INNS OF BANFF PARK

CREAMY TRUFFLES

makes 40 to 50

chocolate, semi-sweet or milk	1 lb (450 g)
whipping cream	1 cup (250 ml)
Grand Marnier, Kahlua, Amaretto, Tia Maria or other liqueur	½ oz (15 ml)
dipping chocolate, cocoa, or icing sugar	½ oz (15 ml)

Finely chop chocolate and melt gradually in a double boiler; keep warm. Whip whipping cream until it holds a peak. Add warm chocolate to cream and stir vigorously until well mixed. Stir in liqueur and cool in refrigerator. When cold, beat until fluffy. Spoon out small mounds and roll small pieces in the palm of your hand. Dip in chocolate or cover in cocoa or icing sugar.

YE OLDE FUDGERY

MELISSA'S FAMOUS BRAN MUFFINS

yields 12-7¼ oz (210 g) muffins

bran	3 cups (750 ml)
brown sugar	1¼ cups (330 ml)
raisins	2 cups (500 ml)
dates	1 cup (250 ml)
baking powder	3 tsp (15 ml)
baking soda	2 tsp (10 ml)
salt	1 tsp (5 ml)
cinnamon	2 tbsp (30 ml)
milk	4 cups (1 l)
eggs	3
vegetable oil	5 oz (150 ml)
vanilla extract	1 tsp (5 ml)
molasses	3 tbsp (45 ml)
flour	2 cups (500 ml)

In a large bowl, combine all dry ingredients. In another bowl, beat milk, eggs, oil and vanilla extract together at medium speed. Add the dry ingredients to the milk mixture, add molasses, and beat for 3 minutes.
Pour the batter into greased chicken pot pie tins (or muffin pans for smaller muffins) and bake at 450°F (230°C) for 30 to 40 minutes or until done.

MELISSA'S MISSTEAK
RESTAURANT & BAR

"The Banff boys who went to Calgary last week to enlist in the South African Constabulary changed their minds and came back."

Banff Crag and Canyon, Mar. 4, 1901

TARTE AUX POMMES
(Apple Tarts)

makes one 9 inch (23 cm) tart

short crusty pastry	**10 oz (300 g)**
medium sized apples, peeled and wedged	**5**
sugar	**4½ oz (130 g)**
milk	**1⅓ cups (330 ml)**
35% cream	**2 cups (500 ml)**
egg	**1**
cinnamon	**¼ tsp (1 ml)**
vanilla	**1 tsp (5 ml)**

Line a 9 inch (23 cm) tart or pie pan with pastry ⅛ inch (3 mm) thick. Poke pastry with fork. Arrange apple wedges on pastry shell and sprinkle with 3 oz (80 g) sugar. Bake at 400°F (200°C) for about 20 minutes until almost done.

Combine and thoroughly mix the milk, cream, egg, cinnamon, vanilla and most of the remaining sugar. Strain. Pour this custard mixture over apples in tart shell. Return to oven and bake about 20 minutes longer. Sprinkle with sugar when pie is still hot.

Beat Maeder
Chef
POST HOTEL

" 'I wish to complain', said the bride haughtily, 'about that flour you sold me, It was tough'.
'Tough, ma'am?' asked the grocer.
'Yes tough. I made a pie with it and my husband could hardly cut it'."

Banff Crag and Canyon, Aug. 24, 1912

ALMOND TORTE

makes one ten inch (25 cm) torte

eggs	**4**
sugar	**1¼ cups (300 ml)**
almonds, untoasted	**1 cup (250 ml)**
flour, sifted	**3 tsp (15 ml)**
baking powder	**2½ tsp (12 ml)**
almond extract	**2 tsp (10 ml)**
whipping cream	**1½ cups (375 ml)**
cocoa powder	**¼ cup (60 ml)**
vanilla	**2 tsp (10 ml)**
coffee	**1 tsp (5 ml)**
salt	**¼ tsp (1 ml)**
Swiss Almond liqueur	**4 tsp (20 ml)**
fresh roasted almonds, sliced	

Beat eggs and ¾ cup (175 ml) sugar until smooth.
Grind almonds. Add almonds, flour and baking powder
to egg and sugar mixture. Beat until smooth. Blend in almond
extract. In greased 10 inch (25 cm) pan, bake at
325°F (170°C) for about 40 minutes.
Whip whipping cream with remaining ½ cup (125 ml) of
sugar until thick. Add cocoa, vanilla, coffee and salt.
Continue beating until mixture forms stiff white peaks.
Fold in liqueur to complete frosting.
Frost cake and garnish with sliced almonds.

SUNSHINE VILLAGE SKI
AND SUMMER RESORT

Facing page: Heli-skiing Deep Powder
Scott Rowed Photograph

APPETIZERS, SAUCES & SPECIAL DRESSINGS

'You did ask for something special!',
Fanny Fowles in costume, 1912
Byron Harmon Photograph

CONTENTS

Featured in other sections:

LE MOUSSELIND DE SAUMON CHANTILLY
(Salmon Mousse with Scampis)

makes twelve appetizers

fresh salmon, cleaned and deboned	18 oz (500 g)
whipping cream	14 oz (400 ml)
egg whites	4
lobster butter	1½ oz (50 g)
Hollandaise sauce	10 oz (300 ml)
Icelandic scampis	12
vegetable broth	18 oz (500 ml)
Worcestershire sauce	
lemon juice	
salt	
butter	

*Very thoroughly grind the salmon and place in a bowl
on ice. Whip the cream and mix with salmon. Beat the egg
whites until stiff and fold into salmon mixture. Season to
taste with Worcestershire sauce, lemon juice and salt and
place in 12 well buttered molds. Place filled molds in a
large pan about half filled with water and poach in oven at
325°F (165°C) for 12 to 15 minutes.
While poaching the salmon mousse, boil the peeled scampis
in the vegetable broth for about 5 to 6 minutes. Melt the
lobster butter and combine with the Hollandaise sauce.
To serve, remove the salmon mousse from form and place on
plate or platter. Place a scampi on top of each and top
with lobster Hollandaise sauce. Garnish with parsley or
fresh dill.*

Gerhard Frey
Chef
LE BEAUJOLAIS

*"Seventeen young ladies, selected by popular vote as the most
beautiful in Seattle . . . were in Banff . . . and some of them were
so careful of their beauty that they would not bathe at the Cave and
Basin because the swimming suits did not include stockings!
Good thing Aphrodite didn't come ashore on the North Pacific coast."*

Banff Crag and Canyon, June 24, 1905

BUMPER'S HOUSE DRESSING

makes three cups (750 ml)

Italian dressing	**2 cups (500 ml)**
cold water	**¾ cup (185 ml)**
egg, hard boiled, chopped coarse	**1**
feta cheese, crumbled	**1 oz (30 g)**
shrimp, chopped coarse	**2 oz (60 g)**
Worcestershire sauce	**1 tsp (5 ml)**
soya sauce	**1 tsp (5 ml)**
Tabasco sauce	**5 drops**

Thoroughly mix all ingredients in a bowl and chill in refrigerator.

**BUMPER'S
THE BEEF HOUSE**

*"The Rocky Mountain Bighorn soon may become milady's latest pet
. . . While it may enjoy bounding from precipice to precipice . . .
the tamed sheep . . . can be taught little tricks . . . and not
only do them for the caretaker but for any visitor. All folks look
alike to sheep, once tamed."*

Banff Crag and Canyon, May 25, 1928

CABOOSE SNAPPY HOUSE DRESSING

makes about one pint (500 ml)

vegetable oil	1 cup (250 ml)
onion, grated	1 tbsp (15 ml)
Parmesan cheese, grated	2 tbsp (30 ml)
salt	2 tsp (10 ml)
dry mustard	1 tsp (5 ml)
black pepper	1 tsp (5 ml)
sugar	1 tsp (5 ml)
Worcestershire sauce	1 tsp (5 ml)
red wine vinegar	½ cup (125 ml)
lemon juice	1 tbsp (15 ml)

Put oil, onion, cheese, salt, mustard, pepper, sugar and Worcestershire sauce in a blender and blend for about 30 seconds. Add vinegar and lemon juice and blend for another 10 seconds.
An ideal dressing for green vegetables which can be stored for several days in a refrigerator.

CABOOSE
STEAK AND LOBSTER

"*It is one of the incongruities of the beauty search that women will spend the greater part of an hour before their glass, attempting to aid nature in her good intentions and conceal her little malices, only to destroy the whole carefully built structure by frowns and grimaces . . . This is done in a mistaken effort to appear serious, perhaps to give an impression of deep thought and mental gymnastics . . . (but) all the world is aware brains are not dependent upon facial contortions.*"

Banff Crag and Canyon, May 25, 1912

CABBAGE-ASPARAGUS TART APPETIZER

serves eight

phyllo pastry	1 package
unsalted clarified butter	4 oz (115 ml)
bread crumbs	
onion, diced	½
fresh parsley, chopped	½ cup (125 ml)
cooked ham, chopped	1 cup (250 ml)
fresh mushrooms, chopped	16 oz (450 g)
butter	2 tbsp (30 ml)
cabbage, chopped	4 cups (1 l)
asparagus, trimmed and cut into 1 inch (2.5 cm) pieces	8 oz (225 g)
cream cheese	8 oz (225 g)
dill	1 tsp (5 ml)
thyme	½ tsp (2 ml)
eggs	4
salt	
pepper	

Cook cabbage until done and cook asparagus until tender crisp. Drain well.
Sauté onions, parsley, ham and mushrooms in butter.
Add cabbage and asparagus. Beat eggs and mix together with softened cream cheese and herbs. Add to skillet mixture, stir thoroughly and set aside.
On a round flat 9 inch (23 cm) pizza pan, lay down 4 square sheets of phyllo pastry so that the sheets overlap in the centre and extend over the pan's edge. Brush with clarified butter and sprinkle with bread crumbs. Repeat this with 3 more layers, alternating the pastry sheets to completely cover the pan with sheets extending over all edges. Put the cabbage mixture in the centre of this arrangement and spread out evenly to about 1 inch (2.5 cm) from the edge of the pan. Fold the extended pastry over the cabbage mixture to overlap in the centre. Top with a few more phyllo sheets and brush with butter. Cut top layer into 8 pie shaped portions with a serrated knife. Bake at 350°F (180°C) for about 1 hour.

Lynne Grillmair
Chef
Bugaboo Lodge
CANADIAN MOUNTAIN HOLIDAYS

SCALLOP AND MUSHROOM APPETIZER

serves four

olive oil	1 tbsp (15 ml)
onion, finely chopped	¼ cup (60 ml)
garlic cloves, minced	2
Bay scallops, rinsed and trimmed	16 oz (450 g)
fresh parsley, chopped	2 tbsp (30 ml)
thyme, crumbled	½ tsp (2 ml)
dried hot chili pepper, seeded and crumbled	1
fresh mushrooms, sliced	2 cups (500 ml)
cognac	2 tbsp (30 ml)
dry white wine	¾ cup (185 ml)
tomato sauce	½ cup (125 ml)
cornstarch	1 tbsp (15 ml)

Heat oil in a skillet and sauté onions with garlic until transparent. Add scallops and sauté gently, then remove. Add mushrooms, parsley, thyme and pepper. Sauté. Return scallops to skillet.
Heat cognac in a large saucepan. Then add wine, tomato sauce and juices from scallop and mushroom mix. Add cornstarch and boil for about 5 minutes. Add scallops and mushrooms. Simmer until heated through. Serve on shells or small dishes.

Lynne Grillmair
Chef
Bugaboo Lodge
CANADIAN MOUNTAIN HOLIDAYS

"Roy Beavers will serenade the Karnival Kween at the ice maze with his favourite song, "Sweet Adeline." This is a very late one and probably has never been heard around these parts before, at least not the way Roy sings it."

Banff Crag and Canyon, February 7, 1923

MUSHROOM ROULADE WITH HAM MOUSSE FILLING

serves fourteen as an appetizer

Mushroom Roulade

fresh mushrooms	1½ lb (675 g)
eggs	6
butter	½ cup (125 ml)
salt	½ tsp (2 ml)
pepper	¼ tsp (1 ml)
lemon juice	2 tbsp (30 ml)
vegetable oil	
parsley, chopped	

Brush a 10 inch (25 cm) jelly roll pan with oil.
Line with wax paper and brush with oil. Set aside.
In 3 batches, chop the mushrooms very fine in a
food processor. Place in a tea towel, roll up, and squeeze
out the juice.
Separate eggs. Beat yolks until fluffy. Add yolks, butter
(melted), salt, pepper and lemon juice to mushrooms.
Beat egg whites until soft peaks form and fold into the
mushroom mixture.
Pour into prepared pan, spread evenly, and bake at 350°F
(180°C) for about 15 minutes or until sponge begins to pull
away from the sides of the pan. Turn out on to towel
sprinkled with parsley.

Ham Mousse

cooked ham, finely chopped	12 oz (340 g)
cream cheese, softened	8 oz (225 g)
sour cream	½ cup (125 ml)
butter, softened	4 oz (115 g)
Dijon mustard (optional)	1 tbsp (15 ml)

MUSHROOM ROULADE WITH
HAM MOUSSE FILLING (Continued)

*Beat cream cheese and butter together. Then gently stir
in ham, sour cream and mustard.
Spread ham mousse evenly on mushroom roulade. Roll up
and refrigerate for 3 to 4 hours before slicing and serving.
Serve on a small plate and garnish with spinach leaves,
Calamata olives and toast points that have been dipped
in melted butter, Parmesan cheese, and baked at 400°F
(200°C) for 10 to 15 minutes, turning over half way through
- until crisp.*

*Lynne Grillmair
Chef
Bugaboo Lodge
CANADIAN MOUNTAIN
HOLIDAYS*

EGGS 'LAC MIROIR'

*Fry one inch square slices of ham in butter, add stewed
tomatoes. Let simmer for five minutes then break eggs into it.
Season and bake together in the oven until the
eggs are cooked.
Mr. Anderegg named this dish after the beautiful
Lake Mirror that nestles in the clouds above Lake Louise.*

*Caspar Anderegg
Chef
CHATEAU LAKE LOUISE, 1930
reprinted from
Banff Crag and Canyon,
August 22, 1930*

*". . . the Banff Literary-Dramatic Club . . . was quite annoyed at
certain individuals who persisted in laughing and snickering during
the presentation of 'The Riders of the Sea' — a most dramatic
play, depicting the morbid customs of the Irish fisher folk . . ."*

Banff Crag and Canyon, April 24, 1923

'SPANIKAPITA' HOT APPETIZER

makes twelve to fifteen appetizers

spinach, fresh or frozen	16 oz (450 g)
eggs	2
feta cheese, crumbled	8 oz (225 g)
garlic clove, freshly minced	½
Parmesan cheese, grated	¼ cup (60 ml)
salt	
black pepper	
nutmeg	
phyllo pastry	1 package
egg wash	
butter, melted	

Cook fresh spinach or thaw frozen spinach. Drain completely, squeezing all water out and finely chop. Mix thoroughly with eggs, feta cheese, Parmesan cheese, garlic, salt, pepper and nutmeg to taste.
Take 1 phyllo sheet, brush with melted butter and fold in half lengthwise. Place about 1 to 2 tbsp (15 to 30 ml) of filling in the lower corner and fold in a triangular fashion, continuing to fold until you reach the end of the pastry sheet. Place on a baking tray and brush with egg wash. Continue making these individual 'pitas' until filling is gone. Bake at 350°F (180°C) for 20 to 30 minutes or until golden brown.

Jaroslav Nydr
Executive Chef
CHATEAU LAKE LOUISE

"Some misguided men in the United States have the idea that their wives boss their incomes . . ."

Banff Crag and Canyon, November 12, 1912

SOUR CREAM TOPPING

covers one nine inch (23 cm) cake

sour cream	**2 cups (500 ml)**
sugar	**1 cup (250 ml)**

*Mix and stir until sugar is completely dissolved. Let stand
for about an hour before using.
An ideal topping for cheesecakes.*

ORANGE SAUCE

sour cream	**2 tbsp (30 ml)**
orange juice concentrate	**3 tbsp (45 ml)**
whipped cream	**1 cup (250 ml)**

*Stir sour cream and orange juice concentrate together.
Then fold in whipped cream. Add more orange juice
concentrate if stronger flavour desired. Serve with
Zucchini Bread (recipe page 72).*

CHATEAU LAKE LOUISE

*"I am told to consult carefully a food-value list . . . for the good of
my health . . . Maybe if I did, I'd live to be a hundred . . .
Unfortunately, the camper is too busy to puzzle it out: one has to
go fishing."*

Elon Jessup, 1924, in 'Camp Grub'

SAUCE TOMATO

fish velouté	1⅔ cups (400 ml)
tomato purée	2 oz (60 g)
or	
fresh tomatoes, peeled	7 oz (200 g)
garlic clove, crushed	1 (small)
butter	1 oz (30 g)

In a small pot, add the tomato and garlic to the fish velouté. Cook gently for about 15 minutes. Strain through fine sieve, season to taste, and add butter and stir in. Serve with fish.

Jaroslav Nydr
Executive Chef
CHATEAU LAKE LOUISE

LAKE LOUISE SPECIAL SAUCE

To be served with crab salads or shrimp cocktails. To one pint of very thick mayonnaise add one hard-boiled egg chopped finely, one finely chopped red pimento, one teaspoon of fresh coarse ground white pepper, one soup spoon of Tarragon vinegar and one soup spoon of Chili Sauce. Add chopped parsley and chives with salt and pepper to taste.

Caspar Anderegg
Chef
CHATEAU LAKE LOUISE, 1930
reprinted from
Banff Crag and Canyon,
August 22, 1930

BAGNA CAUDA
(Spanish Vegetable Fondue)

recipe proportional to number served

salted butter	**1 part**
olive oil	**1 part**
anchovies, mashed	**$\frac{1}{10}$ part**
garlic cloves, pressed	**$\frac{1}{10}$ part**

In a heavy fondue pot, melt butter and add anchovies, garlic and olive oil. Let simmer on low heat for 20 minutes.

For vegetable plate:
broccoli
cauliflower
zucchini
tomato
fresh mushrooms
onions

Slice broccoli, cauliflower, zucchini and mushrooms into bite sized chunks. Slice tomatoes into wedges (or use cherry tomatoes) and onions into rings. Arrange on plate and serve with fondue.

Louis Lanthier
Chef
THE GRIZZLY HOUSE

"Crowds thronged the sidewalks and parking spaces for autos were difficult to find at times."

Banff Crag and Canyon, May 25, 1928

SALSA

whole peeled tomatoes	28 oz (800 ml) can
jalapenos	6 oz (170 ml) can
tomato	8 oz (225 ml)
green (unripened) tomatoes	8
onions, peeled and chopped	2
green peppers, chopped	2
fresh parsley	1 bunch

*Combine all ingredients in a blender or food processor
and blend until a smooth purée.
Salsa is an excellent dip for corn chips, can be used to add
zest to vegetables and meat, and is used in Huevos Rancheros
(see recipe, pg. 66).*

MAGPIE & STUMP

MELISSA'S HONEY-MUSTARD DRESSING

makes 1¼ cups (300 ml)

water	3 tbsp (45 ml)
vegetable oil	½ cup (125 ml)
vinegar	4 tbsp (60 ml)
red wine	2 tbsp (30 ml)
honey mustard (available commercially)	4 tbsp (60 ml)

*Mix ingredients in a sauce pan and stir frequently over
low heat until honey mustard is completely dissolved.
Let cool and serve.*

*MELISSA'S MISSTEAK
RESTAURANT & BAR*

NEW YORK STYLE CHICKEN WINGS

serves proportionally to number of chicken wings

Lightly deep fry chicken wings. Eat with fingers and serve with Blue Cheese Sauce:

mayonnaise	8 oz (225 ml)
sour cream	8 oz (225 ml)
paprika	3 tbsp (45 ml)
garlic, minced	1 tbsp (15 ml)
cumin seed, ground	2 tbsp (30 ml)
blue cheese, crumbled	8 oz (225 g)
salt	
pepper	

Mix thoroughly.

*MOUNTAIN GREENERY
RESTAURANT AND
DANCE CLUB*

LOBSTER SAUCE

fish velouté (white fish sauce)	2 cups (500 ml)
whipping cream	½ cup (125 ml)
lobster, diced	4 oz (115 g)
lobster butter (or base)	4 oz (115 ml)
paprika	2 oz (60 g)

In small pot, mix together fish velouté, whipping cream and paprika. Bring to boil and boil until total mixture is reduced to about 2 cups (500 ml), then strain. Remove from heat, beat in lobster butter and stir in diced lobster. Serve with Omelette 'Gourmet'. (See recipe pg. 38).

*C. Allan Winder
Executive Chef
RIMROCK INN*

CREVETTE COCKTAIL

serves two

jumbo gulf shrimp, pre-cooked or boil in salt water until shell is pink	4 oz (115 g)
long English cucumber, diced ¼ inch (5 mm)	2 oz (60 g)
tomato, blanched and seeded, diced ¼ inch (5 mm)	2 oz (60 g)
white vinegar	2 tbsp (30 ml)
olive oil	4 tbsp (60 ml)
fresh dill	
salt	
white pepper	
shredded lettuce	
slice of hard boiled egg	
tomato wedge with meat removed	
slice of black olive	

Slice shrimp in half and place in bowl. Add diced cucumber and tomato and freshly chopped dill. Add vinegar and olive oil and salt and pepper to taste.
Arrange the mixture on a bed of shredded lettuce either on a small plate or in a champagne glass. Garnish with a slice of hard boiled egg, a tomato wedge and a slice of black olive.
If you use a champagne glass, rub the rim of the glass with a wedge of lemon and dip the rim in chopped parsley.

C. Allan Winder
Executive Chef
RIMROCK INN

Facing page: Afternoon at Lake Minnewanka
Douglas Leighton Photograph

DRINKS, HOT & COLD

'Something for the bar'
Byron Harmon Photograph

CONTENTS

GLACIER COFFEE

Grand Marnier	½ oz (15 ml)
Kahlua	½ oz (15 ml)
Amaretto	½ oz (15 ml)
coffee, hot	¾ cup (185 ml)

Moisten rim of glass with lime and dip in sugar.
Serve topped with whipped cream and maraschino cherry.

HOT APPLE PIE

dark rum	¾ oz (22 ml)
Amaretto	¾ oz (22 ml)
apple juice	2 oz (60 ml)
apple cider, hot	4 oz (115 ml)
cloves	sprinkle
nutmeg	sprinkle
cinnamon	sprinkle

Serve in hot drink glass topped with whipped cream
and a fresh apple slice.

BANFF PARK LODGE

"I put in all my conscience will allow and then add a bit more."

on making camp coffee, 1924,
Elon Jessup in 'Camp Grub'

MOUNTAIN MIST

Swiss Chocolate Almond liqueur	**½ oz (15 ml)**
peppermint schnapps	**½ oz (15 ml)**
coffee, hot	**4 oz (115 ml)**

Serve topped with whipped cream.

COURTSIDE COOLER

vodka	**1 oz (30 ml)**
cranberry juice	**2 oz (60 ml)**
soda water	**2 oz (60 ml)**
lime mix	**dash**
peppermint schnapps	**'a hint'**

Serve in a tall glass on ice.

BANFF ROCKY MOUNTAIN RESORT

"In the true chef's tradition he threw pots and pans around the kitchen, hurled carving knives at helpers, and, one day, reaped all he had sown . . . (in a rage and) Brandishing a large spoon he . . . vaulted over the top of the counter — to land with great ceremony right in the middle of 360 dessert dishes of jello, each topped with whipped cream and one-quarter of a maraschino cherry."

description of 1920's chef Robert, by Bart Robinson, in his 'Banff Springs — The Story of a Hotel', Summerthought Ltd., Banff, 1973.

HOO DOO

Southern Comfort	1 oz (30 ml)
vodka	1 oz (30 ml)
orange juice	½ oz (15 ml)
lime juice	½ oz (15 ml)
peppermint schnapps	splash
Sprite	splash

Build and serve in a zombie glass garnished with
orange slices and a maraschino cherry.

BON VOYAGE

tequila	1 oz (30 ml)
Southern Comfort	1 oz (30 ml)
Amaretto	½ oz (15 ml)
Triple Sec	1½ oz (45 ml)
pineapple juice	to taste
orange juice	to taste

Build on crushed ice and serve garnished
with orange slices and a maraschino cherry
in a lip swirl glass.

GLACIER TODDY

Kahlua	½ oz (15 ml)
Grand Marnier	½ oz (15 ml)
Bailey's Irish Cream	½ oz (15 ml)
fresh cream	2 oz (60 ml)

BANFF SPRINGS HOTEL

ROCKY MOUNTAIN SUNRISE

tequila	¾ oz (22 ml)
Amaretto	½ oz (15 ml)
orange juice	3 oz (85 ml)
Grenadine	dash

Serve in a tall frosty glass on ice.

GREEK BANANA

rye	1 oz (30 ml)
brandy	1 oz (30 ml)
Creme de Bananes	½ oz (15 ml)
dark cacao	½ oz (15 ml)
apricot brandy	½ oz (15 ml)
Galliano	½ oz (15 ml)
fresh cream	6 oz (170 ml)

*Blend or shake on ice and serve
in 16 ounce champagne glasses.*

DOCTOR DEATH

Kahlua	¾ oz (23 ml)
Grand Marnier	½ oz (15 ml)
Benedictine	½ oz (15 ml)
Chartreuse	¼ oz (7 ml)
coffee, hot	to taste

Serve in a brandy snifter and top with whipped cream.

*BUMPER'S
THE BEEF HOUSE*

AVALANCHE

white rum	1 oz (30 ml)
Galliano	½ oz (15 ml)
apricot brandy	½ oz (15 ml)
pineapple juice	to taste
orange juice	to taste

*Blend and serve in a tulip glass
with pineapple chunks, orange slices and
a maraschino cherry (with a long straw).*

STRAWBERRY GLACIER

white rum	1½ oz (45 ml)
strawberry concentrate	2 oz (60 ml)
strawberries, frozen	2 oz (60 ml)
lime mix	to taste
crushed ice	2 scoops

*Blend thoroughly and serve in a jubilee glass
garnished with fresh strawberry or lime
with doily spoon and plate.*

TERRACE COOLER

Coconut Rum	1¼ oz (35 ml)
pineapple juice	to taste

*Build over ice and serve with assorted fruit
and a swizzle stick.*

CHATEAU LAKE LOUISE

HOT MULLED WINE

water	1½ cups (375 ml)
sugar	7 oz (200 g)
ground nutmeg	1 pinch
ground allspice	1 pinch
cinnamon	1 pinch
ground cloves	1 pinch
molasses	3 tbsp
oranges	2
Triple Sec	26 oz (750 ml)
red wine	

*Bring water to boil and dissolve
in sugar to make syrup. Stir in spices
and molasses and keep warm.
Peel oranges with vegetable peeler.
Chop the zest (orange peel) finely and blanch
in boiling water. Add zest to syrup mixture
and let cool.
Strain juice from oranges and add to
syrup mixture. Stir in 1 bottle of Triple Sec
and let stand at room temperature for 1 day.
(Will keep indefinitely; use as desired)*

To serve Hot Mulled Wine:

*Slowly heat syrup mixture. Add red wine
(1 part syrup to 3 parts wine; California Mountain
Burgundy suggested), stir gently, and heat
until warm. Serve in warmed mugs or glasses.*

DEER LODGE

*"It should be understood that the mattresses on the Bankhead rifle
range were placed there for the use of the club members when
shooting, and for no other purpose."*

Banff Crag and Canyon, August 11, 1906

SCHI WASSER

Kirsch	1¼ oz (37 ml)
raspberry syrup	¾ oz (22 ml)
lemon juice	
hot water	

CELESTIAL REBOUND

Southern Comfort	1 oz (30 ml)
Kahlua	½ oz (15 ml)
Amaretto	½ oz (15 ml)
apricot brandy	½ oz (15 ml)
pineapple juice	

Shake well and serve.

STEAMBOAT

Kahlua	¾ oz (22 ml)
Creme de Cacao	½ oz (15 ml)
coffee, hot	

Serve topped with whipped cream.

GRIZZLY HOUSE

"It provokes a coolness if a girl sees a man, who is quite a masher, in the daytime, bristly, bald, fat, puffing . . . it may be a glimpse into married life for the girl . . ."

Douglas Sladen, 1895, in his
'On the Cars and Off

INN'S SPECIAL

brandy	1 oz (30 ml)
Kahlua	½ oz (15 ml)
Creme de Cacao	½ oz (15 ml)
coffee, hot	
cream	

STRAWBERRY GRANDE
(Marguerita)

tequila	1¾ oz (50 ml)
Triple Sec	¼ oz (7 ml)
shaved ice	¼ cup (60 ml)
lemon juice	dash
lime juice	dash
bar sugar	1 tbsp (15 ml)
fresh strawberries	6

INNS OF BANFF PARK

" 'I have a profound respect for bacon', remarked a thoughtful citizen
. . . 'Did it ever occur to you that we are indebted primarily to bacon
for the opening up and development and civilization of this great
and glorious West? That without bacon, this grand country, with . . .
all its . . . wonderful evidences of progress and prosperity . . . would
probably be a howling wilderness at the present moment?'

The thoughtful citizen paused for a breath.

'You astonish me', said his friend across the table."

from editorial 'Bacon and Civilization'
Banff Crag and Canyon, Feb. 18, 1901

ROCKY MOUNTAIN BUMPSUCKER

Southern Comfort	1¼ oz (35 ml)
white vermouth	splash
ginger ale	

HORSE'S NECK

| scotch | 1¼ oz (35 ml) |
| ginger wine, to taste | |

JOSHUA'S
RESTAURANT & PUB

"The private distiller or moonshiner, call him which you will, was a wise and cautious man and had a habit of burying his surplus stock . . . along the banks of Whiskey Creek. The liquid joy, no matter how it was distilled, should be almost priceless now . . . whoever unearths (this) buried treasure should, in common humanity, donate a small portion (a gallon or two) to the editor of this journal — to be used for scientific purposes."

Banff Crag and Canyon, 1916

WINE MARGUERITA

twenty servings

dry white wine	2 qts (2 l)
water (or soda water)	½ qt (500 ml)
can of limeade concentrate	12½ oz (355 ml)
fresh limes	12
lime mix	9 oz (250 g)
Triple Sec	7 oz (200 ml)

*Combine water, limeade concentrate, lime powder
and juice squeezed from limes. Stir briskly
until dissolved. Add wine and Triple Sec, cover
and refrigerate for at least 1 hour before serving.
To create a frothy marguerita combine the whites
from 2 eggs with 6 servings of the marguerita
and whip in a blender for 2 or 3 minutes.*

MAGPIE & STUMP

*"Much annoyance has been caused to one of Banff's business men
by an unfounded story that he had supplied brandy to a laundry
woman who was discharged from a local hotel for drunkeness. The
liquor was obtained from another hotel on the plea that she needed it
for a sick friend."*

Banff Crag and Canyon, June 25, 1912

MELISSA'S PEPPERMINT PATTI

peppermint schnapps	1 oz (30 ml)
hot chocolate	6 oz (170 ml)
whipped cream	

*Pour hot chocolate and schnapps into a
wrapped snifter or mug, stir together well,
and top with whipped cream.*

MELISSA'S FROZEN
STRAWBERRY MARGUERITA

crushed ice	1½ cups (375 ml)
frozen strawberries, thawed	⅓ cup (80 ml)
tequila	1 oz (30 ml)
Triple Sec	¼ oz (7 ml)
lime mix	3 oz (85 ml)

*Put all ingredients into a blender and blend
at medium to high speed for about 20 seconds
or until mix is smooth and slushy.
Pour into a wide long-stemmed glass,
garnish with a lime wedge, and serve with a straw.*

*MELISSA'S MISSTEAK
RESTAURANT & BAR*

*"Rev. Father Macdonald declares that Ike Mills' racing team is not
composed of prohibition dogs as they show a fondness for light whines."*

Banff Crag and Canyon, February 7, 1923

BLUEBERRY TEA

Grand Marnier	¾ oz (22 ml)
Amaretto	½ oz (15 ml)
tea, hot	

Serve in a snifter.

KAMIKAZEE SHOOTER

vodka	¾ oz (22 ml)
Triple Sec	¼ oz (7 ml)

Serve in a shooter glass. Good luck!

***THE MOUNTAIN
GREENERY RESTAURANT
AND DANCE CLUB***

"The ignorant imbecile who contributed the Banff items to the (Calgary) Albertan of Saturday's issue may be surprised that his identity is well known, and his cowardly remarks regarding the lady members of the Banff Quadrille Club will but intensify the supreme contempt in which he is already held. The editor of this paper will take pleasure in assisting the ladies to administer to this sneaking reptile the only punishment his miserable apology for a soul is capable of appreciating — a good horse-whipping."

Banff Crag and Canyon, Feb. 2, 1901

LAST RUN

Amaretto 1 oz (30 ml)
hot chocolate 6 oz (170 ml)

*Serve topped with whipped cream and garnished
with an orange slice, a maraschino cherry,
and a fruit stick.*

BEAUTIFUL COFFEE

Grand Marnier ½ oz (15 ml)
Courvoisier ½ oz (15 ml)
coffee, hot 6 oz (170 ml)

*Serve topped with whipped cream and garnished
with an orange slice and a maraschino cherry.*

POLAR BEAR

Grand Marnier 1 oz (30 ml)
Kahlua ½ oz (15 ml)
coffee, hot 6 oz (170 ml)

*Serve topped with whipped cream and
garnished with an orange pinwheel.*

*SUNSHINE VILLAGE SKI
AND SUMMER RESORT*

TICINO SPECIAL

brandy	¾ oz (22 ml)
Galliano	½ oz (15 ml)
lemon juice	

TICINO SWISS—ITALIAN
RESTAURANT

CAFE DIABLO

brandy	¼ oz (7 ml)
Demerara rum	½ oz (15 ml)
Amaretto	½ oz (15 ml)
coffee, hot	

Moisten rim of glass with orange slice
and dip in sugar. Serve topped with whipped cream
and a cinnamon stick.

THE YARD

"The initial moonlight trip to Lake Minnewanka . . . 60 ladies and
gentlemen started out from the King Edward Hotel . . . in Tally-hos,
democrats, and buggies, a small orchestra also going out . . . (to)
the old chalet for supper . . . after which dancing kept up till
it was time for the return journey, home being safely reached
shortly after two a.m."

Banff Crag and Canyon, June 25, 1912

Facing page: Winter moonrise over Mount Rundle
and Vermilion Lakes.
Douglas Leighton Photograph

A DINING GUIDE

'A party (without this guide)
looking for a good restaurant',
on Resplendent Mountain, 1913
Byron Harmon Photograph

DINING GUIDE

"Man is a social animal, he loves to get in bunches of his own kind, and when . . . people see that big crowds are coming to Banff, they say to themselves 'the people are going to Banff . . .', and away they go.

Banff Crag and Canyon, September 15, 1917

BALKAN VILLAGE RESTAURANT

*Specializing in authentic gourmet Greek cuisine, the cozy
Balkan Village Restaurant is the latest hot spot on Banff's
dining scene. Delectable lunches and dinners, a warm,
cheerful atmosphere and friendly staff in traditional
Greek garb (not to mention the occasional belly dancer!),
make the Balkan Village a taste of the Mediterranean
in the heart of the Rockies.*

Open daily 11 a.m. to 11 p.m. Lunch 11 a.m. to 4 p.m.

120 Banff Avenue; 762-3454

BANFF PARK LODGE

*The Terrace Dining Room in the Banff Park Lodge invites
you to enjoy fine dining under the stars. The glass skylight
and elegant decor set the scene for friendly service
and excellent continental specialties prepared to delight
and satisfy the most discriminating palate.*

Open 5 p.m. daily. Reservations are recommended.

222 Lynx Streeet; 762-4433

BANFF ROCKY MOUNTAIN RESORT

*With a dazzling view of Cascade Mountain, D. B. Dowling's
Restaurant and Lounge is at the heart of Banff's newest
resort complex. A cozy bistro style restaurant, it is open
for breakfast, lunch and dinner and offers everything
from Bow River Submarines to pâtés and Chicken Dijon.
The intimate lounge features evening entertainment.*

Open daily 7 a.m. to 11 p.m. Dinner reservations suggested.

*Junction of Banff Avenue and
Tunnel Mountain Road;
762-5531*

BANFF SPRINGS HOTEL

*Towering above the pine forests along the Bow River,
the grand old Banff Springs Hotel evokes the spirit
of European aristocracy. Within this 'castle of the Rockies'
is a community of dining spots as diverse and cosmopolitan
as her visitors.
Reflecting the hotel's baronial Scottish look, the
Rob Roy Room offers traditionally elegant dinner cuisine
and evening dancing. A diverse table d'hôte menu
featuring Spanish specialties, complemented by grand decor
and evening dancing, is the forte of the Alhambra Room.
(An à la carte breakfast is also featured.) Prime Alberta beef
highlights the varied dinner menu of the Alberta Room,
where breakfast and lunch diners are greeted with a
superb buffet. For something completely different, enjoy the
authentic Japanese Sushi and Shabu-Shabu Bar at the
Samurai Restaurant. Drop in at Grapes Wine Bar for wine,
cheese and light snacks, the Van Horne Room for a
continental breakfast or an afternoon tea, or the desserts
and specialty coffees of the Cafe Expresso. In summer,
enjoy barbecue treats on the Red Terrace overlooking
the valley. And just a few minutes from the hotel,
The Clubhouse above the golf course offers
tasty breakfasts and lunches.*

Open daily. Dinner reservations are suggested.

Spray Avenue; 762-2211

LE BEAUJOLAIS

*It could perhaps be said that it is scrupulous attention to
detail that has made Le Beaujolais one of western Canada's
premier restaurants: the gracefully elegant decor,
garnished with such touches as a single long-stemmed rose
on every table; the table side service, in the finest
French tradition; the elaborate menu of gourmet cuisine,
skillfully prepared from only the finest and freshest
ingredients; and the tastefully selected wine list,
featuring Beaujolais varieties seldom seen in Canada.
It all comes together to create a classic dining experience,
praised as a 'Restaurant fit for a king' and recommended
in the prestigious 'Where To Eat In Canada'. Your hosts,
Albert Moser and George Schwarz, wish you "Bon Appetit!"*

Open daily 5 p.m. to 11 p.m. Reservations required.

Banff Avenue at Buffalo Street; 762-2712; 762-5365

BUMPER'S THE BEEF HOUSE

Serving more dinners than any other restaurant in town, the motto at Bumper's The Beef House is "If you haven't been to Bumper's, you haven't been to Banff". Featuring a menu starring their famous Alberta beef prime rib and giant Bumper's Bar-B-Que Ribs, an 'all you can eat' salad bar, and moderate prices. The evening entertainment and ski movies and fun, friendly feeling top off this popular dining experience.

Open daily for dinner 4:30 p.m. to 10 p.m. with a lighter menu served until 11 p.m.; breakfast served, summer only, 7 a.m. to 10 a.m.; lounge open 4:30 p.m. to midnight (to 1 a.m. Friday and Saturday).

Next to Bumper's Inn,
Banff Avenue and Marmot Street; 762-2622

CABOOSE STEAK AND LOBSTER

Situated in the CPR railway station, the Caboose Steak and Lobster is a unique dining room where you can enjoy delicious Alberta prime beef, steaks, lobster, crab legs, and Rocky Mountain trout surrounded by fascinating railway memorabilia. Dip into the hearty salad bar served from a converted porter's cart. Casey's Lounge adjacent. Ample parking. Recommended by AAA and CAA.

Open daily from 5 p.m. to midnight.

Junction of Elk and Lynx Streets; 762-3622 or 762-2102.

CANADIAN MOUNTAIN HOLIDAYS

As home base for heli-skiers enjoying the ultimate untracked powder snow experience or heli-hikers savouring the spectacular alpine scenery, the Bugaboo Lodge is an oasis of warm hospitality and gourmet home cooking in the heart of the remote Bugaboo Mountains. With ingredients brought in by helicopter, the ever changing, innovative and international cuisine makes dining at the lodge the perfect complement to each exhilarating day in the mountains.

Open winter for heli-skiing, summer for heli-hiking.

Canadian Mountain Holidays,
P.O. Box 1660, Banff, Alta., T0L 0C0; 762-4531

CHATEAU LAKE LOUISE

Overlooking one of the world's most famous landscapes, the Chateau Lake Louise offers a variety of dining spots in a grand and palatial setting. The new Tom Wilson Rooftop Restaurant features relaxed breakfasts, lunches and dinners at moderate prices (and an awe inspiring view at no extra cost!) Complete with a massive stone fireplace, a mounted moose head and arched windows looking out over the lake, the spacious Victoria Room offers breakfast and lunch buffets and a fine table d'hôte dinner menu. For formal dining with elegant service and decor, try the Fairview Dining Room and their new gourmet seafood specialties. In the cheerful Poppy Room, family fare at family prices is the specialty. The casual Glacier Lounge (featuring outdoor patio service in summer) and the more formal Lobby Lounge are the spots for light meals and evening entertainment. For pizza, sandwiches and salads, there's Dick Turpin's Pub, Deli and Pizza Parlour and outdoors in summer enjoy light snacks on the Poolside Terrace. And for the early birds, don't miss the dawn light on the Victoria Glacier while enjoying the 6 a.m. Summer Sunrise Breakfast served in the lobby.

The Chateau is open daily with varying hours for specified restaurants. Reservations for dining are recommended.

At the lake, Lake Louise; 522-3511

DEER LODGE

After over 60 years of summer service, Deer Lodge, 'the real mountain lodge at the lake', now extends its warm welcome to winter visitors as well. Just a 3 minute stroll from the shore of Lake Louise, the log lodge offers accommodation, entertainment, and relaxing views of the Victoria Glacier from its roof-top hot tub. In the elegantly rustic Cafe Louise, the creative cuisine and gracious service capture the spirit of the mountains. Enjoy afternoon tea and capuccino or a late night cocktail in the original Lake Louise Trading Company teahouse. In summer, the DeliCafe offers light meals and the Ice Cream Parlour offers delicious treats.

Open daily with breakfast buffet 7:30 a.m. to 10 a.m. and dinner served 6 p.m. to 10 p.m. Lounge open 11 a.m. to 12 p.m.

At the lake, Lake Louise, 522-3747

YE OLDE FUDGERY

One of Banff's most unique and popular shops.
Over 20 varieties of delicious creamy fudges, brittles,
"snails", candy and caramel apples, truffles and much more —
all made daily while you watch (and smell!).

Open summer season 8 a.m. to 11 p.m. and 10 a.m. to 6 p.m.
throughout the year with weekend opening till 9 p.m.
Mail orders are accepted.

The Sundance Mall, 215 Banff Avenue; 762-3003

GIORGIO'S

Giorgio's is actually two restaurants in one but both
specialize equally in offering some of the best home-made
pasta dishes this side of Italy. Upstairs, the classy
La Casa features elegant dining and a full selection of
meat, fish and pasta dishes prepared in the tradition of
northern Italy. The more casual La Pasta offers gourmet
pasta and pizza dishes to delight any palate and pocketbook.
A truly memorable dining experience.

La Pasta is open daily 4:30 p.m. to 11:30 p.m.
La Casa is open daily 5:30 p.m. to 10 p.m.
Reservations are required for La Casa.

219 Banff Avenue; La Casa; 762-5116; La Pasta; 762-5114

GRIZZLY HOUSE

The fun of fondue dining at its best is the specialty
of the Grizzly House and the warmth of the natural wood
decor and the friendly and casual atmosphere create the
ideal setting. A choice of 11 fondues, ranging from
traditional Swiss Neuchatel to Buffalo and accompanied by
a variety of tasty sauces, makes this spot a real playground
for the palate. Steak, chicken and veal sausage entrées
and a variety of appetizers round out the dinner menu.
A daily luncheon special is also featured.

Open daily 11:30 a.m. to 11 p.m.

207 Banff Avenue; 762-4055

INNS OF BANFF PARK

*Set in the circular centerpiece of the Inns' dynamic
architecture, the Reflections dining room offers a varied
à la carte dinner menu of fine beef, poultry and seafood
dishes, complemented by elegant French service, a mellow
tropical decor and a spectacular mountain panorama.
Skier's breakfast and dinner specials are also featured
in season. And above Reflections, a carved wooden bear
greets visitors to the solarium style Belvedere Lounge
for evening entertainment.*

Open daily. Dinner reservations are appreciated.

600 Banff Avenue; 762-4581

JOSHUA'S RESTAURANT & PUB

*Excellent food complemented by friendly service and a
warm elegant atmosphere is Joshua's successful dining
formula. The decor of this cozy restaurant features
fine old-English furniture, Victorian window panes
and chandeliers made from old gas lamps. Even the friendly
waitresses are dressed in a style reminiscent of a
grander era. Start with appetizers like escargot, caviar,
smoked oysters or Russian eggs before delicious entrées
like prime rib, seafood, or Tournedos À La Joshua's,
complete with home-made soup or a garden fresh salad;
and all for attractively moderate prices. Top the
evening off with a stop at Joshua's Pub.*

*Open daily from 5 p.m. to 10 p.m. Pub open noon to midnight.
Restaurant reservations recommended.*

204 Caribou Street; 762-2833

MAGPIE & STUMP

*With a well earned reputation for serving some of the
best gourmet Mexican dishes in western Canada, the
Magpie & Stump is one of Banff's most popular restaurants
and nightspots. A refurbished old saloon building
featuring rustic weathered wood and a sprinkling of
wild west memorabilia and curiosities — including,
of course, a magpie and stump — provides the setting;
and the friendly staff and evening entertainment
creates the warm relaxed atmosphere so suited to the fare.
For those with less adventurous palates, steak, chicken
and pizza are also offered.*

Open daily 5 p.m. to 2 a.m.

203 Caribou Street; 762-2014

MELISSA'S MISSTEAK RESTAURANT & BAR

*Offering great food and a relaxed atmosphere, Melissa's
serves more meals than any other restaurant in Banff.
Housed in the rustic log original Homestead Hotel, it
offers fun and family food at reasonable prices. Featuring
such delights as their acclaimed 'made-from-scratch' giant
bran muffins, their tuna fish bagel, and their thick crust
deep dish pizza to filet mignon dinners, Melissa's popularity
is well deserved. Upstairs, the stand-up bar offers free
popcorn, games, TV, cheap drinks and plenty of good times.*

*Open daily 7 a.m. to 11:30 a.m. for breakfast, 7 a.m. to 4:30 p.m.
for brunch, 11:30 a.m. to 4:30 p.m. for lunch, 4:30 p.m. to 10 p.m.
for dinner and 10 p.m. to 11 p.m. for their Late Night Menu.
Bar open noon to 12:30 a.m.*

*Across from the Banff Park Lodge, 218 Lynx Street;
762-5511.*

THE MOUNTAIN GREENERY RESTAURANT AND DANCE CLUB

At home in the original 1920's Cascade Dance Hall (complete with spring loaded floors), the Mountain Greenery offers a warm and cheerful atmosphere amidst lush plants, stained glass and a California style decor. Innovative cuisine is the order of the day for breakfasts, lunches and dinners. In the evening, when the lights are dimmed and the music brings the old dance floor to life, the Nite Bites menu offers appetizing finger foods galore.

Open daily 8 a.m. to 1:30 a.m., except winter when only open to 10 p.m. some evenings. Dinner served until 10 p.m.

120 Banff Avenue; 762-5000

POST HOTEL

Originally built as a warm home base for visiting mountaineers, the Post Hotel has a long history as a meeting place where adventurers from the Alps came to discover the Rockies. Today, this tradition lives on in the warm European atmosphere that prevails and the gourmet cuisine carefully created by their Swiss chef to be reflective of both the Rockies and their topographical soulmates, the Alps. The best of Canadian dishes prepared in the finest Swiss tradition. Afternoon Tea Time, featuring fresh cakes and home-made fruit pies, is a memorable treat. The innkeepers, George Schwarz and Barbara and Andre Schwarz, wish you "Bon Appetit!"

Open daily 2 p.m. to 5 p.m. for Tea Time and 5 p.m. to 10 p.m. for dinner. Reservations are recommended.

Lake Louise; 522-3989

RIMROCK INN

*Perched high above Banff on the side of Sulphur Mountain,
the Rimrock Inn's Eagle's Nest Dining Room offers
quality cuisine in a breath-taking mountain setting.
A varied dinner menu of creative à la carte house specialties
offers something to delight every palate. Breakfast and lunch
are also served and the Sunday Champagne Brunch, served
from 11 a.m. to 2 p.m. has become a famous local dining event.*

*Open daily, with variable serving times through the seasons.
Reservations are suggested.*

*Mountain Avenue (beside the Sulphur Mountain Hot Pools
and the Sulphur Mountain Gondola); 762-3356*

SUNSHINE VILLAGE SKI AND SUMMER RESORT

*Surrounded by the peaks and alpine meadows of the Great
Divide, Sunshine Village sits 'on top of the world'. From
November to June, it is the most popular ski resort in the
Rockies; and with its new summer operation, it is fast
becoming a favourite destination for those with a taste for
summit scenery and fresh mountain air. To match these
mountain high appetites, the Eagle's Nest Dining Lounge in
the Sunshine Inn offers a varied menu of hearty breakfast,
lunch, and dinner selections. And after dinner, the
entertainment in the Trapper's Lounge or a free guided
nature walk through the meadows rounds off an enjoyable
evening in the mountains.*

*Open daily in season 7 a.m. to 10 p.m.
Reservations are requested.
Accessible only by a scenic 3 mile (5 km) gondola ride.*

*P.O. Box 1510, Banff, Alta., T0L 0C0; 762-4000;
1-800-372-9583, Alta. Toll Free Reservations;
1-800-661-1363, Canada/USA Toll Free Reservations*

TICINO SWISS-ITALIAN RESTAURANT

*The southernmost province of Switzerland, Ticino is
a land of mountain pastures and vineyards where the
Alps meet the plains of northern Italy. The merging of
Swiss and Italian culture here has produced a distinctive
cuisine — a cuisine prepared with traditional care here
in the Rockies by the Ticino Swiss-Italian Restaurant.
Milk-fed veal, beef and cheese fondues, steaks and
pasta dishes are the specialties and your hosts,
Hermann Zehnder and Erwin Widmer, take pride to
ensure that each is prepared and served to both your
satisfaction and theirs. The price range is moderate
and soup and salad are included.*

Open daily 5 p.m. to 11 p.m. Reservations recommended.

205 Wolf Street; 762-3848

THE YARD

*An old lumber yard reborn as a cozy restaurant, The Yard
is one of Banff's newest dining spots. Texas slow-smoked
barbecue and gourmet Mexican dishes, an easy going
atmosphere and moderately priced dining are the specialties.
And weather permitting, you can enjoy all this, plus a
Mt. Rundle view, on the street side garden terrace.*

*Open daily 7:30 a.m. to 3:30 p.m. for breakfast and lunch
and 5:30 p.m to 11 p.m. for dinner.*

206 Wolf Street; 762-5678

The Perfect Memento of Your Stay.
The Perfect Gift For Those You Wished Were Here.

Please send _____ copies of **A TASTE OF BANFF**

Name _____

Street _____

City _____

Postal/
Province/State _____ Zip Code _____

Enclosed find $9.95 per copy plus $1.00 for postage and handling.
(Total $10.95 per copy).

Total of Money Order $

Payable to: A TASTE OF PUBLISHING INC.
P.O. Box 25
Banff, Alberta, Canada
T0L 0C0

Please send _____ copies of **A TASTE OF BANFF**

Name _____

Street _____

City _____

Postal/
Province/State _____ Zip Code _____

Enclosed find $9.95 per copy plus $1.00 for postage and handling.
(Total $10.95 per copy).

Total of Money Order $

Payable to: A TASTE OF PUBLISHING INC.
P.O. Box 25
Banff, Alberta, Canada
T0L 0C0

The Perfect Memento of Your Stay.
The Perfect Gift For Those You Wished Were Here.

Please send _____ copies of **A TASTE OF BANFF**

Name _____

Street _____

City _____

Province/State _____ Postal/ Zip Code _____

Enclosed find $9.95 per copy plus $1.00 for postage and handling. (Total $10.95 per copy).

Total of Money Order $

Payable to: A TASTE OF PUBLISHING INC.
P.O. Box 25
Banff, Alberta, Canada
T0L 0C0

Please send _____ copies of **A TASTE OF BANFF**

Name _____

Street _____

City _____

Province/State _____ Postal/ Zip Code _____

Enclosed find $9.95 per copy plus $1.00 for postage and handling. (Total $10.95 per copy).

Total of Money Order $

Payable to: A TASTE OF PUBLISHING INC.
P.O. Box 25
Banff, Alberta, Canada
T0L 0C0

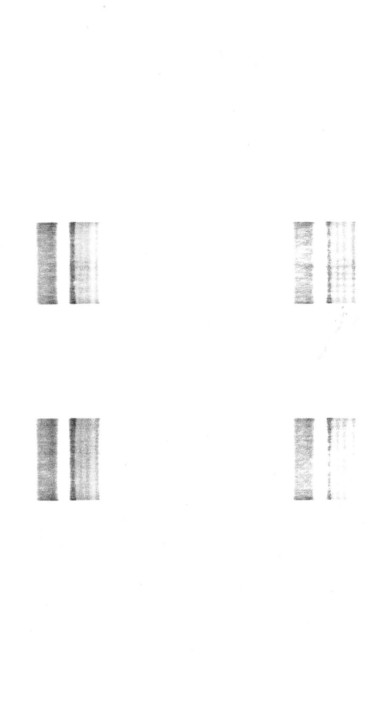